MADDEN HILLS

BACK-
TO-BASICS
MANAGEMENT:

The Lost Craft of Leadership

BACK-TO-BASICS MANAGEMENT:

The Lost Craft of Leadership

Matthew J. Culligan
Suzanne Deakins
Arthur H. Young

Illustrations by Dick Ross

FACTS
ON FILE

460 Park Avenue South, New York, N.Y. 10016

Back-to-Basics Management:
The Lost Craft of Leadership

Matthew J. Culligan, Suzanne Deakins and Arthur Young

Copyright © 1983 by Matthew J. Culligan

Published by Facts On File, Inc.
460 Park Avenue South, N.Y., N.Y. 10016

Library of Congress Cataloging in Publication Data

Culligan, Matthew J., 1918–
  Back to basics management.

  Includes index.
  1. Management. I. Title.
HD31.C82 1983   658   82-18196
ISBN 0-87196-755-3

Printed in the United States of America

10 9 8 7 6 5 4 3 2 1

Table of Contents

Preface

Some very fundamental concepts can be drawn from the many hints, ideas and techniques suggested throughout this book.

First and foremost, the authors' focus centers on the individual—on the individual manager and the proper management of other individuals. This is because it is our deeply felt belief that the key factor in motivation, productivity, profit and successful management is the individual. No matter what the job, the work situation is always the same: a private encounter between the individual and his or her task. Any change which influences this central relationship for the better can—and will—be truly significant in terms of corporate results.

That is the essence of back-to-basics management. There are dozens and dozens of books available on management principles, motivation, productivity, understanding how corporations function and hints on how to get along in the corporate structure. But the authors firmly believe there is much more to successful managing than principle, theory and the "bottom line." We believe that people are the "X" factor. People in business are the dynamic variable—capable of amazing feats or of living and working in the kind of day-to-day drudgery that has unfortunately become the accepted norm.

It was not always so. The old "Mom and Pop" operation may not have been run by sharp buyers and producers, and they were anything but bottom line-oriented, but they knew their people. They knew what turned them on, they knew how they differed and they knew how to motivate them. What's more, they worked at working with them—directing them, growing with them, gaining participation, building feelings of responsibility and involvement through consistent delegating. In short, they managed people to achieve corporate results.

Essentially, that is our definition of "back-to-basics-management." It's a restatement of the importance of human values. It's a recognition that working through people is the key function of managers. It's an awareness that goal setting will be more realistic and achievable if put in the context of individual needs and wants.

No, it is not a wishful desire to turn back the clock to the "good old days." It is not a soft-hearted approach to management. It is not idealism and theory. Rather, it is a hard, penetrating look at reality in business today. The sweeping social changes affecting all of us and the attitudes and work habits of managers are not taking place in separate worlds. They are interwoven. They are inseparable. They are the roots of effective management today.

Easy? No! What we are suggesting is a very basic and, at the same time, a much higher form of management. One that immeasurably alters and expands the role of the managers today. One that places heavy emphasis on an understanding of the behavioral sciences *and* the particular aspects of any and all job functions. One that is, in reality, a form of management demanding more skills and a broader outlook on the part of the manager.

Introduction

BACK-TO-BASICS MANAGEMENT was written largely because the three authors, each of whom has had extensive experience in and with management, came to the same conviction regarding what they saw as one of the key problems in American business today.

What we are concerned with is the phenomenon known as the "MBA mentality." This, in our opinion, is a wonderfully simplistic way of looking at the complexities of modern business. Planning is important; organization is important; goal-directed behavior is important; bottom-line awareness is important. *But* these are only the beginning, because all the numbers and rules are subject to change when you run up against the great variable—*people.*

Coupled with the growing dependence on "planners" rather than "doers" is the enormous change resulting from the rapid rush into computerization. Here too the emphasis has been on facts and figures which seem to represent a higher truth because they come out of a complicated and *expensive* electronic brain. How soon we forget the first law of computerization: Garbage in, garbage out.

Since both computers and the "MBA mentality" are largely the province of the young, they have lead to still another problem—a developing generation gap in business and industry. Were it not for the liquidity crisis in the late 1960s and early 1970s and the current recession, the MBAs and computer experts might well have totally dominated management. But these times of crisis painfully illuminated the essential weaknesses of process-oriented managers and inexperienced MBAs. When sales declined and costs skyrocketed, profits and stock prices went down and down. It was then that chief executive officers turned to their pragmatic, experienced, people-oriented managers to solve their problems. It was back-to-basics management in full flower.

We do not mean to turn back the clock. Nor do we in any shape, manner or form intend to demean the thousands of bright, able, hard-working young managers in the country. Rather we want to help them by focusing their attention on the "people" aspects of their job. Helping people communicate better, listen better, manage their time better, set higher goals and be more strongly motivated to reach those goals *is* "the bottom line."

In his many years as an economist and college professor, George Schultz, our current Secretary of State, made this point many times. He espoused a practical philosophy stressing the importance of the human resources of the United States. The key, he explained, was not the manufacturing, distribution and selling of products. It was not mining, construction, transportation or the communications media. Rather it was the level of intelligence, skill and dedication and the caring and sharing of *people* which made the difference.

Back-to-basics management concerns itself with the best use of these human resources. It is a key step on your path to managerial excellence. We urge you to keep this foremost in your mind as you read, use and, we hope, enjoy this book.

BACK-TO-BASICS MANAGEMENT:

The Lost Craft of Leadership

CHAPTER ONE

What Is Back-To-Basics Management?

We live in a credential-happy age. A few letters after our name are regarded as reasonably good evidence that we know what we are doing. Nowhere is this more apparent than in American business. During the past two decades three ordinary letters have been transformed into a magical spell that, like "open sesame," can open the heaviest doors without effort. An MBA has become the key to the executive suite.

Many people assume that an MBA is a certified expert in management. Yet, even the words behind the magic letters do not imply this. Business administration sounds mundane and *is* a rather static concept. On the other hand, while management sounds fairly mundane, business has long regarded it as a dynamic concept. An administrator presides over a business; a manager leads it.

A principal theme of this book is that this seemingly semantic difference is of enormous significance to the future of business. We have filled the top echelons of our corporations with administrators who *preside* over the entities they ought to lead. By an overemphasis on process and techniques, we have lost the craft of leadership.* How did this come about? With typical American exuberance, U.S. businesses and industries went "overboard" in willy-nilly acceptance of computers when they proved their great utility to scientists, engineers and accountants. Scientists, engineers and accountants were the first sponsors of adding machines and calculators, and it followed that they would also be among the first to recognize computers as a great boon in the gathering, storage and retrieval of information. Computers made possible in minutes calculations which previously took teams of accountants days and weeks to complete.

Then the cost of computers became a matter for top management consideration, and applications to other parts of business and industry were considered. The Fortune 500 companies plunged into computerization at enormous expense, and smaller businesses soon followed suit. There was a dangerous side effect. Most of the top executives of U.S. corporations during the 1960s and early 1970s had an ignorance of mathematics and an abhorrence of electronics. They were forced to turn to process-oriented specialists and to MBAs in an attempt to get control of the monsters they themselves had created. Virtually every graduate of the good business schools was recruited and employed by Fortune 500 companies and the smaller corporations that follow the leaders. Management information systems became the vogue, and it was anticipated that the great IBM would develop the complete integrated management information system based on its own computers. It came as a great shock to IBM and the rest of the industry when it was learned that even IBM could not accomplish that goal.

There was another shocking revelation during the liquidity crisis of the late 1960s and the early 1970s. During the long bull market, which convinced all Wall Streeters that they were geniuses, MBAs evolved impressive looking programs in long-range financial planning using computers. These were presented to top management and caused some euphoria. A typical plan showed the various sources of financing available to a corporation when it needed to borrow money. The banks were delighted to give loan guarantees and loan commitments, and

* This is not to say, of course, that the holder of an MBA cannot be a manager-leader. Theoretically, the percentage of potential manager-leaders among MBAs should be similar to the percentage among businessmen and women with an equal number of years of business experience. In reality, MBAs as a group probably produce fewer manager-leaders because they have to overcome their initial misconception that a business consists of numbers rather than people.

investment bankers courted the large corporations tendering their services in public offerings and private placements. Because none of the MBAs were old enough to remember the deep recession and depression days, they never realized that the statements of bankers and investment bankers in prosperous times have no validity in recessions and depressions. The loan commitments and loan guarantees melted away in the heat of the liquidity crisis. While most of the big corporations survived, many smaller ones did not. There was a general communications failure between the pragmatic top management and the MBA management of the middle and lower levels.

Business and industry recovered from the liquidity crisis: memories were short, and the overdependence of top management on computers and MBAs again developed. We will not belabor the issue, preferring to use examples, analogies and aphorisms where possible to make specific points. For example, the American business executive with the highest favorable visibility as this book is written is Lee Iacocca, the president of the Chrysler Corporation. Rudely fired by Henry Ford II because, as Ford put it, "I never liked him," Iacocca was immediately hired by Chrysler Corporation, which was on the brink of bankruptcy. Iacocca, a former "whiz kid" of the McNamara team at Ford, has that rare combination of creative and administrative skill. He moved decisively after gaining comprehension of the problems of Chrysler and presented plans to congressional committees to justify the loan guarantees which saved Chrysler. During a period of some relaxation and reflection, after the major crisis was over, Iacocca was asked about MBAs in business and industry. He replied, "MBAs know everything but understand nothing."

The authors of this book perceived deep meaning and significance in this remark. We believe it provides a tremendous insight into what has gone wrong with American companies in their fascination with "method" rather than understanding.

We started at the root of the problem by attempting to define the essential difference between "knowing" and understanding. We delved deeper and, after many hours of thought and discussion, we evolved this formula, which we offer as a foundation block for back-to-basics management:

News + information + comment   = knowledge
Knowledge + thinking + feedback = understanding

We paused at that point, moderately satisfied that we had synthesized two rather amorphous concepts and the difference between them. But then we realized that even understanding, in a sterile, "ivory tower" ambiance, was not the final answer. So we took our formula one step further:

$$
\begin{aligned}
\text{News + information + comment} &= \text{knowledge} \\
\text{Knowledge + thinking + feedback} &= \text{understanding} \\
\text{Understanding + commitment + discipline} &= \text{back-to-basics} \\
&\quad\ \text{management}
\end{aligned}
$$

With a deep bow in the direction of Lee Iacocca for stimulating the thinking and feedback, we proceeded with this formula as foundation block number one of back-to-basics management.

It became apparent that foundation block number two had to be effective communication. The computer is the ideal instrument for the gathering, storage and retrieval of news, information and comment, which make up the body of knowledge. The process-oriented technicians and the MBAs are needed for this function, but during the thinking and feedback stage, higher levels of pragmatic thinking are required to convert the acquired knowledge into understanding. Since MBAs recently graduated from business schools are virtually identical in their mental processes, it is obvious that there is very little value in their talking to each other. That is like hitting a tennis ball against a blank wall; it's good practice, but it's not like a real game.

Foundation block number three of back-to-basics management flows logically from the first two foundation blocks. It recognizes that each human being is a combination of mind, body and emotions and must be considered in the light of that immutable fact. Since each group is a combination of individuals, then the group is the sum of the minds, bodies and emotions of all. We have labeled foundation block number three interpersonal relations. To review, back-to-basics management is based on:

$$
\begin{aligned}
\text{Foundation block number one} &= \text{understanding + commitment} \\
&\quad\ \text{+ discipline} \\
\text{Foundation block number two} &= \text{effective communication} \\
\text{Foundation block number three} &= \text{interpersonal relations}
\end{aligned}
$$

There are many subdivisions of these three foundation blocks which can, in a sense, be looked on as a three-leaf clover.

No one work can do everything, so we have devoted much time to the addenda material, particularly the Bibliography. We will put heavy emphasis on learned skills. We urge you to make the important concepts in this book a part of your nature, guiding you in your thinking patterns, your understanding of management principles and your increasing sensitivity to interpersonal relations and humane, compassionate person-to-person management. Can the writers of this book do that? Emphatically not! We need another expert who knows more about you, what makes you tick, what turns you on, what are your major strengths and weaknesses. Who's this big talent we're going to call on to help? Surprise! You!

That's right. One of the ways in which awareness is achieved is through the mechanism of intellectual intimacy. While many books focus on learning how to understand others, we feel a valid experience is possible by following the Socratic mandate, "Know thyself!" The back-to-basics manager must understand and come to terms with his

own values and practices before the behavior of others assumes its real significance. Through the process of synthesis you will then be able to understand your own behavior and the behavior of the people in your group. It is in this way that you will be able to learn what kind of actions and practices on the part of different individuals contribute to or detract from the goal of organizational excellence.

We hope that this book, and your continuing study through life will provide an opportunity for you to put all the pieces of the human puzzle together so that they may acquire an integrated conceptual foundation for your own development as a manager.

The lifetime business objective of the manager is to achieve clear awareness of himself, his family and neighbors and those over whom he has management responsibility. The other side of that equation is that the manager must always strive to avoid self-deception and self-delusion. Clear awareness is the result of a continuing process of study and observation. For example, if you spent your life at street level in a major city, your world would be limited by what you could see and hear, touch and smell at street level. If you moved to higher levels your world would expand. The higher the level you achieve, the larger the overview of interrelationships.

It also follows that the higher the level of overview you can achieve early in your career, the more certain you can quickly advance over your contemporaries who have not sought your loftier overview. This is not a quality which has to be paraded or illustrated. The individual with a high overview will generally not make spot judgments on insufficient data or facts. ("Shooting from the hip" is not appreciated in modern business.) The way you perform in meetings and in written responses during the normal course of business will not be lost on your superiors. You will gradually be perceived as capable of the long view and as an outstanding prospect for advancement.

At this juncture the authors will practice what they preach where overview is concerned. Our overview of the back-to-basics manager led us to the conclusion that the following characteristics are essential.

1. *The back-to-basics manager knows himself. He can . . .*
   - Define who he is and where he wants to go
   - Set goals and objectives
   - Set realistic priorities
   - Project a leadership image
   - Recognize areas of weakness and seek to overcome them

- Channel his energy towards objective self-appraisal and superior performance.

2. *The back-to-basics manager is an expert at getting things done. He can...*
   - Identify obstacles, blockages, habits and conflicts
   - Develop the ability to manage change—including changing technology, changing markets and changing attitudes
   - Implement specific programs to increase productivity.

3. *The back-to-basics manager is skilled in time management and self-organization. He can...*
   - Recognize and avoid unproductive and time-consuming tasks
   - Delegate tasks and cut out time-wasters of all kinds
   - Take inventory of his personal organization and that of his department.

4. *The back-to-basics manager understands the use of communication as the prime management tool. He can...*
   - Be aware of and constantly improve his listening, speaking and writing skills
   - Gather as many facts as possible in an organized and objective manner
   - Exchange information skillfully and effectively
   - Enhance morale by telling subordinates the "why" of a decision rather than just the "when" and "how"
   - Communicate what's expected in an objective and persuasive manner
   - Use persuasive language to gain support for his ideas and opinions.

5. *The back-to-basics manager is big on people skills. He can...*
   - Motivate the people he interacts with every day
   - Devise strategies for working with and getting more out of people
   - Implement action plans for dealing with people
   - Encourage each subordinate's growth and independence without a feeling of being threatened
   - Use praise and criticism judiciously to let others know exactly how he responds to their work

- Develop techniques to encourage efficiency
- Utilize the most effective methods of teamwork, with emphasis on maximum group interaction
- Understand conflict—and how to deal with it.

6. *The back-to-basics manager is creative and innovative—and knows how to motivate and use the creative output of his group. He can...*
   - Remove internal blocks to creativity for himself and the people with whom he works
   - Turn fact-finding skills into directed creativity
   - Shape ideas into solutions
   - Understand group creativity and make the process work
   - Select the most useful solution from the many ideas generated
   - Translate this solution into practical terms and specific strategies
   - Win support for his ideas and put them into action.

7. *The back-to-basics manager knows how to delegate work successfully. He can...*
   - Give employees the independence they need for job satisfaction
   - Spell out accountability in specific, measurable terms
   - Match delegated tasks with abilities
   - Free his own time so he can better concentrate on planning and supervision
   - Monitor performance in a way that avoids employee frustration
   - Encourage subordinates to make decisions on their own.

8. *The back-to-basics manager knows how to be an effective supervisor. He can...*
   - Orient new people to their jobs quickly and effectively
   - Train new people to be productive in a short space of time
   - Plan work for maximum productivity
   - Handle grievances and difficult employees
   - Share in the formulation of short- and long-term goals.

In these turbulent times there are no easy answers for businesses or individuals. The road that leads to back-to-basics management is full of challenges. You cannot expect to sit in a classroom and become a back-to-basics manager and a leader overnight. It will take determination and constant awareness of yourself. There are many areas to understand and to which to tailor your own personality. There is no way to tell you how you will know when you are successful; only careful review of your activities and the results will tell you that. You must start by understanding that as a back-to-basics manager your major resources are your employees. Now a moment of philosophical thought as we end this chapter. Consideration of the other individual in one-to-one situations and consideration of group attitudes and characteristics are essential to positive relationships. Even if there cannot be agreement, the knowledge that there has been consideration of contrary viewpoints will almost always make it possible for the other party or parties to accept decisions. But there cannot be consideration without what we call creative listening. The habit of creative listening will enrich your business and personal life. We dare to say that you can not truly be a back-to-basics manager without creative listening.

CHAPTER TWO

Creative Listening

"Filling our ears with all we have learned to say,
we are deaf to what we have yet to hear."
Wendell Johnson

Putting this chapter near the beginning of this book signals our belief that listening is essential to back-to-basics management and the craft of leadership. There can be little argument that when the mouth is open and the tongue is wagging, the ears are closed.

It is widely believed that business loses an enormous amount of money each year because of ineffective listening. Assuming that each person on the work force makes only a ten-dollar listening mistake once a year, it is easy to estimate the cost to business: One billion dollars!

Ineffective listening by management at all levels can be disastrous to a corporation's profit. Poor listening results in outmoded products, union and employee problems, lost clientele, unsatisfied customers, just to mention a few of the consequences. A recent research project in a large sales organization showed that 4 out of 5 client complaints could be traced directly to ineffective listening skills by salespersons and managers.

Research shows that the manager-leader spends approximately 70% of his day in some form of communication. Forty-five percent of that time is spent listening. An ineffective listener can forget as much as

75% of what he has heard within 24 hours. He may only be able to retain and relate to as little as 50% of what he hears at the moment of listening. A good percentage (at least 25%) of the conversation can be forgotten in as little as 3 to 4 hours. Many managers and leaders may by functioning on as little as 10% of the information they receive.

Back-to-basics management and leadership demands effective listening. What is so difficult about listening? For one thing there is a great difference between the rate of speech (about 125 words per minute) and the rate at which the brain can operate (between 400 and 500 words per minute). It is therefore an effort to listen attentively. There will always be a tendency to interrupt if you sense where the speaker is taking you. The mind can wander and even worse, for this can be insulting, the eyes can drift away from the speaker. It is a rare human being who was not actually conditioned *against* some listening during childhood. Most of us have heard "don't listen to him" or "we don't listen to such things in this family" or "don't pay any attention to him."

If given a choice, most managers will choose a speaking course above a listening course. A poor speaker learns of his difficulties quickly when he sees his audience start to fall asleep. But listeners are in the best position to check up on themselves. Unless someone has a hearing problem, it seems difficult to believe that listening is a learned skill. One of the most common misconceptions about listening is the notion that because we can hear we are listening.

What Is Listening?

Receiving audible stimuli is similar to receiving light through your eyes. In themselves, neither noise nor light has any particular meaning. Until you give them meaning, they remain noise or light. The process of receiving and processing noise and translating the sounds into agreed-upon symbols is called hearing.

Listening is a selective process by which we choose the specific audible stimuli surrounding us, based on our needs and our purposes. We listen and "lock in" to stimuli:

- Because they are sudden, intense or contrasting
- Because we have trained ourselves to listen for them
- Because this is automatic in nature.

As a manager this may become clearer if you will observe the change in your listening attention when (1) approached by an employee, (2) approached by a client, (3) approached by your boss.

Listening is a constantly shifting process . . . a kind of hop-skip-and-jump technique. Rather than tuning in completely, we tune in and out on a speaker, listening to see if there is anything we want or need to hear. Human beings have trouble focusing on one stimulus for any length of time. Our antenna is geared, something like a revolving radar scope, to scan the surrounding environment constantly to hear if there is anything of importance or interest to us going on. And that means we are going to miss a lot of what is going on if we are not sufficiently motivated.

Our motivation and feelings have direct impact on our listening effectiveness. We seem to find a message more valuable if we can determine beforehand what information we want from it. Sometimes the inability to focus on a topic is simply a matter of feeling that it does not meet our current needs (i.e., is this information going to deal with the current crisis?). Then we have a tendency to tune out everything else. Psychologists working in this field say we perceive what we want to perceive. That's especially true for listening.

What Prevents Effective Listening?

The five blocks to effective listening are:

- Attempting to extract only the facts from a message. Dealing with facts out of context often causes confusion. It is the full context of a conversation that gives the facts meaning and helps create a clear picture of the circumstances.
- Being emotionally hypersensitive. For many people certain words have a great emotional impact. For example, if a sales manager says to a sales representative, "We lost our California account," the latter may immediately panic. The word "loss" blocks out everything else being communicated.
- Rejection without evidence. Many of us think we know in advance that a subject will be boring or difficult. We close our minds to the subject. Or we listen only to a small portion to reconfirm our preconceptions. We're hearing but not listening.
- Standing at attention. As children, many of us were so often told to pay attention that we developed the habit of looking as if we

were at attention. This fools speakers—but eventually it back-fires in our inability to understand the message being communicated.

- Disliking the "package" and consequently refusing the contents. When we look at a speaker who has distracting mannerisms, or if we don't like the person who is speaking (i.e., an employee with a whiny voice), we have a tendency to criticize the content. Eventually, we stop listening altogether.

Increasing Listening Effectiveness

Basically, effective listening is a matter of getting yourself inside the speaker's head and listening to the message from *his* point of view. Listen to the speaker as if he were speaking to himself. Here's how to increase your listening effectiveness:

- Prepare yourself to listen.
- Listen to the speaker from his point of view.
- Concentrate on the major points and not the facts. This will help you identify important elements and it will give the facts meaning so that you can remember them. Understanding the central idea will increase your memory of the subject being discussed. Concentrate on the content and forget the package. Keep looking for information you can use.
- Build defense mechanisms against words that have emotionally laden meanings for you. Try to hear the meaning the speaker is attaching to a word. Substitute another, less emotive word in your mind for the one that triggers your emotional reaction.
- Learn to keep an open mind. Look for the positive aspects of what is being said. Turn what you feel are negatives into positives.
- Pay attention. Identify the developmental techniques used by the speaker. Note how the talk is organized.
- Keep your mind on the speaker. The relationship between you and the speaker has a great deal to do with your attention and the way you listen. The more we respect the speaker, the more we believe he can influence our lives, the more likely we are to listen. For those you feel are "not worthy," try to remember that they too can have experiences and information which you can make use of. Examine the role and purpose of the speaker. Even

though it may be difficult at times to determine specific roles and purposes, it will help keep your mind on the speaker.

- Listen between the lines for information and ideas that may not have been put into words. Words are accompanied by gestures and expressions that also speak to you—if you listen!
- Try to anticipate points and ideas. Even if your guess is wrong, it will keep your attention focused on the speaker and the subject.
- Review and weigh what you are hearing. This will help keep your mind from wandering.
- Withhold judgment, evaluation and decision until the speaker has finished. Also hunt for ideas that might prove you wrong as well as right.
- Ask mental questions about what is being said. Don't formulate answers and rebuttals immediately. Let the speaker have his say; then you'll have yours.
- Actively seek areas of interest for yourself in what is being said.
- Don't let note taking be a distraction. Notes do not particularly increase listening effectiveness.
- Adjust to distractions; don't just tolerate them.
- Exercise your mind. Learn to listen to technical information and expository material. Good listeners learn to appreciate a wide variety of spoken material.
- Keep eye contact with the speaker (especially on a one-to-one basis).
- Listen with your whole person. You spend a third of your life with your subordinates and superiors. Being able to listen to them and help them is an ability that both you and they deserve.

True listening sometimes means exposing yourself to the fright, rage and depression of another person, and sometimes to the expression of your own deep feelings. It isn't easy. Listening beyond words means understanding the hurts and frustrations. It means helping people to vent their feelings in a constructive manner, rather than shut them off through negativism and criticism. When we listen without judgment, we open lines of communication; we show people we care. (We may not approve of their behavior but our listening behavior can show that we approve of them as people.) Listening is hard work. Research shows that there is an increase in heartbeat and slight increase in temperature. Most people don't want to work at listening. Those who do are well rewarded. Good communication skills and good listening skills show up in bottom-line results. Even more importantly they show in people results.

By breaking down listening skills into groups, we can take a closer look at what actually happens. We suggest that you take one group at a time, work on it, and as you have mastered it move on to the next set of skills. The groups are broken down into three main areas. They are:

- Attention skills: learning how to keep your attention on the speaker
- Direction skills: learning to follow and encourage the speaker
- Reflective and responsive skills: learning to reflect back to the speaker the content, feelings and meaning you have gotten from him.

Attention Skills

Attending is giving your complete physical attention to the person speaking. Listening with your whole body is one way of understanding it. This is the kind of non-verbal communication that lets the person who is talking know that you are paying careful attention. These skills include posture, body motion, eye contact and helping create a non-distracting environment. These skills work wonders with interpersonal relationships.

The body can be positioned so that it encourages, invites and facilitates interpersonal relationships, or it can do just the opposite. A good listener communicates with the body by:

- *Showing relaxed alertness and openness.* You are looking to achieve a balance; a mental state that is saying: "I feel at home with you and accept you. I feel the importance of what you are saying, and I am very intent on understanding you."
- *Inclining the body toward the speaker says* "I am giving support and energy, participating actively." Sitting back and sprawling say, "I don't want to participate." When we hear an exciting public speaker we often say, "He had them on the edge of their chairs."

- *Facing the other person squarely,* shoulder to shoulder. Turning your back or body suggests rejection. Remember the phrase "He gave me the cold shoulder?" That's true—and the speaker will understand it.

- *Positioning himself at eye level with the speaker.* This is especially important if you are an authority figure to the speaker. Not being at eye level puts a barrier to the interpersonal relationship you are trying to achieve.

- *Maintaining an open position with his body.* This demonstrates acceptance, and a lack of defensiveness. You're not closing off the speaker. Don't cross arms and legs—that's a negative sign.

- *Being an appropriate distance from the speaker* is important. Being too far away impedes the conversation, while it also causes tension in the speaker, i.e., you are too far away to be really involved. On the other hand, being too near can also cause anxiety for the speaker. In our American culture the acceptable distance is 3 to 4 feet between speaker and listener.

- *Avoiding rigid body positions.* Body movement is necessary for the speaker to feel involvement on the part of the audience. The listener should be "moved" by what is being said. People prefer speaking to an audience whose bodies are not rigid and unmoving. This doesn't mean a nervous, fidgety type of movement. You should move your body in accordance with the stimuli of the speaker, not the stimuli of the environment that could be distracting.

- *Avoiding distracting gestures and movements.* Drumming your fingers, shifting your weight, crossing and uncrossing your legs and other similar movements reflect nervousness rather than attention.

- *Maintaining effective eye contact. This shows that you are interested* and have a desire to listen. Eye contact is not staring, but rather a soft focusing on the speaker. This includes looking at the speaker, following the speaker's gestures, i.e., shifting from the eyes to his hand movements, then to his other body movements and back to the eyes again. Many people have trouble with eye contact. Their tendency is to look away from the speaker at the first sign of emotion. Part of this is the desire not to intrude, because our eyes can be the most intimate medium of contact we have with another person. No one enjoys having a conversation with someone who is looking around the room. It detracts from the attention you are trying to give the speaker, and the speaker gets distracted from what he is trying to say.

- *Helping to keep the environment from distracting the speaker.* Turn off the radio, close the door, move from behind the desk (especially if you are an authority figure to the speaker). This helps remove the physical barrier between you and the speaker, so he can see your body language and know that you are involved.

- *Maintaining attention. Most important of all a listener must be there psychologically.* Your body language and attending efforts let the speaker know you are *there* and not drifting off somewhere else.

Many of us already have some understanding of the attributes of attention in listening. What we are doing here is making you more aware of precisely what is needed, so you will be able to work consciously on these areas and check on your progress. Most people think of communication as a verbal process. But those who study communication carefully are becoming more and more convinced that it is also a *non-verbal* process.

Direction Skills

One of the primary tasks of the listener is to stay out of the speaker's way so he (the listener) can really hear what the speaker is trying to say. The average listener has a tendency to ask too many questions, or make statements that lead and direct the conversation. Being sensitive to the needs of the speaker should be of primary concern to the listener. Being sensitive to other's needs means knowing when they have the need to speak—and allowing them to speak.

Many of us have had the experience of needing to talk yet having no one to listen. That leads to a feeling of hesitation when we have to speak and unburden ourselves. A good listener can help, by knowing how to open the doors to conversation with non-coercive invitations to talk. Non-verbal clues tell you when someone is burdened or excited. "Door openers" can encourage those who don't seem to be able to speak up. Sometimes a speaker may be in the middle of a conversation when he hesitates; this is a sign that he is unsure about continuing. Through body language and words you can reassure the speaker, letting him know what he needs to say. Too often, instead of opening doors we tend to close them. We give advice or make judgmental statements that keep the person from feeling free to speak.

"Roadblock statements" fall into three categories:

1. *Judgmental statements,* i.e. "What did you do this time?" "Don't be grumpy with me."
2. *Reassuring statements,* i.e. "Cheer up"; "There's always a silver lining."
3. *Advice-giving statements,* i.e. "Why don't you do something you like to do?" "Why don't you go out, sitting inside won't help anything."

"Door openers" have four main elements:

1. *A verbal description of the other person's body language,* i.e. "You look great" or "You look excited."
2. *An invitation to talk or continue to talk:* "Want to talk about it?" "Please go on, I'm interested in what you are saying!"
3. *Silence:* nonverbal nonintrusion that gives the other person a chance to decide whether or not he wants to go on.
4. *Attending:* letting your body language and eye contact say you are interested and have a personal concern for the person.

All four elements may not be present in each door opener. The tone of the relationship, your trust, previous disclosure and your own personality will help determine the nature of the door openers used. The speaker may have difficulty making up his mind to say what he feels. Remember, many people fear disclosure because past experience has taught them it may mean rejection. You can help the speaker surmount the fear of disclosing himself by using door-opening phrases. Door openers should always be an invitation—never a directive—to talk. The empathetic person respects privacy and is careful not to intrude. Honor the speaker's separateness.

When you first start to practice listening skills, you may have a tendency of trying to stay out of the speaker's way and so lapse into non-participation. Instead, try to give low-key encouragement. This means saying very little, but through your body language (a nod of the head that indicates you are listening) and small verbal words (yes!, and? . . . etc.) encourage the speaker to continue. These ideas may also help the conversation to gain momentum. Tone of voice and facial expressions can also be used to convey participation. Encouragement to continue and to talk does not mean that you agree or disagree. You are simply saying, "I am listening and trying to follow your meaning."

Use Questions Sparingly

Questions are a natural part of conversation in our society and culture. Most listeners have the tendency to ask questions directed from the listener's point of view rather than from the speaker's. There are two kinds of questions:

1. Closed-end questions: These demand short specific responses. These "Yes" or "No" type answers leave little or no room for the speakers to explore their answers and express their feelings. They tend to be true/false or multiple choice based on the listener's categories and are the kind of questions that tend to close down the conversation.
2. Open-end questions: These are essay-type questions that encourage the speaker to explore his thoughts and feelings. Open questions do not suggest where the conversation should go next. It is important to ask only one question at a time.

Most of us ask far too many questions in our conversations. Part of this is due to our over-reaction to silence. But questions can put you opposite the speaker rather than with him or her.

Silent responsiveness is often appropriate. Perhaps people feel uncomfortable with silence in a conversation because many of us need someone to listen (and we are always looking for a good listener). Or perhaps silence points out our separateness. So the minute someone takes a breath we tend to start talking. The speaker needs silence in order to gather his thoughts and go deeper into himself. Silent responsiveness does not mean inattention; it actually shows you are participating. The speaker needs to feel he can continue at his own pace without feeling rushed, that silences will not start you talking.

Becoming comfortable with silence and learning what to do during silences eases the feelings of awkwardness. It gives the speaker more confidence, and it makes you a more effective listener.

Reflective and Responsive Skills

The ability to respond to the speaker reflectively is an important part of good listening skills. In a reflective response, the listener's manner demonstrates understanding and acceptance related to the feeling and/or content that the speaker has communicated. Reflective listening and responding has four elements:

- The response is non-judgmental
- The response is an accurate reflection of what the speaker has been experiencing
- The response is concise
- When appropriate, the response reflects more than the words that were spoken.

In reflective responding, the hardest part for the listener is to remain objective. Your feelings and judgments should at no time enter into your response. There are four main ways to respond reflectively:

1.   Paraphrasing is making a concise statement, which states the essence of what the speaker has just said in the listener's own words. In paraphrasing, many people tend to be too wordy. This can sidetrack the speaker's train of thought. Good concise paraphrasing cuts through the clutter of details and goes to the heart of the matter. A good listener develops a sense of what is central to the speaker's message and reflects this back. It is important to note that by putting it in his own words, the listener lets the speaker know he understands what is being said.

   Focus on the content, i.e. facts and ideas rather than emotions, in your paraphrase. Any really distinct line between emotions and facts of course is artificial, but to facilitate understanding (letting the speaker know you are following and getting his meaning) reflection of the content is absolutely necessary. Listeners should be aware of the difference between parroting a speaker's own words and paraphrasing them in the listener's own words. If a listener parrots, he gives the impression he is hearing—but not listening.

2. Reflecting feelings involves playing back to the speaker the emotions he is trying to communicate. When we reflect the speaker's feeling back to him, we are acknowledging the speaker's uniqueness; and our personal reaction to the events and information that have been communicated to us. By reflecting feelings, we allow the speaker to explore his emotions and better understand them, which will help him move closer to a solution. Be careful of questions that elicit fact-type answers and attitudes that say "stick to the facts." If the speaker feels you are not interested in his feelings about a situation he will tend to feel stifled and not free to make further self-disclosures. Remember—feelings are energy forces that help a person sort, organize and implement actions that must be taken. As in all societies, we tend to channel the ways in which individuals are allowed to express their deeply held feelings. Because of this, speakers often have trouble expressing their true feelings about a subject. They tend to "hedge" their feelings, which places the burden of interpretation on the listener. To really understand, the listener must actively participate in the communication process as follows:

• Focus on the feeling words
• Note the central message and content
• Observe the body language of the speaker
• Ask yourself "If I were having this experience how would I be feeling?"

Remember there are no good or bad emotions. Only the actions taken because of emotions can be classified as good or bad.

The speaker will automatically let you know if you have reflected his feelings correctly, and if not, he will correct you. In most cases the speaker will not be distracted by your incorrect reflection. Instead, he will feel good because you have shown him that you care enough to try to understand how he feels.

3. Reflecting meanings happen when the listener brings together facts and feelings in a concise statement, and plays it back to

the speaker. Feelings don't just happen; they are a reaction to an event or situation. It is important to the speaker for the listener to know, not only what his feelings are, but why he is having them. This is best reflected back by combining the feelings and the facts, i.e. "you feel . . . because you. . . . " It is important to note that many times the speaker will not have connected his feelings with the situation. By reflecting back meaning in a concise statement, you will facilitate the conversation. In many conversations, this is often the point at which the speaker will be able to clarify his picture of the problem and begin working on the solution.

Listeners beware! This is the point in many conversations where the speaker will stop talking. He will, in some cases, not let you know he has found a solution. This often leaves the listener with feelings of incompleteness and frustration. Encourage the speaker to continue and verbalize the solution. Most of all accept the fact that many interactions may well be inconclusive.

4. Summary reflections happen when a conversation has gone on for a long period of time, with the speaker having covered a variety of ideas and feelings. This type of reflection helps put fragments of ideas into one meaningful and concise statement, thereby helping the speaker integrate what he has been talking about. Speakers often get lost because of the many confusing thoughts and feelings they have while they are speaking. This summary statement helps put the puzzle together by concentrating on the points that have been stated repeatedly with the greatest intensity. If you leave something out that is important to the speaker, he will let you know. An effective summary will allow the speaker to:

- Speak in more depth
- Make his points with greater coherence
- Understand the total situation more clearly
- Move on towards the next step, or to a conclusion or solution.

In some cases the summary may seem like a whole new idea to the speaker because he has not previously heard all of the relevant data in one concise, non-judgmental statement.

Beyond Reflective Listening

Most people who are effective listeners know that there are often steps beyond reflective listening that can be taken:

- *Additive responses.* These can help the speaker see the world from a more objective point of view. But they can be damaging if the speaker is not ready. Be careful not to give advice. If the speaker has expressed the problem, and you feel a different point of view will facilitate the problem solving, additive phrases can be helpful. Additive responses can be addictive to listeners. The general rule is to let the speaker, as much as possible, come up with a different point of view or a solution.
- *Responding with touch.* There are times when a hug, a pat on the back, or a warm touch, do more for the speaker than anything that can be said. But remember, many people are uptight about any form of physical contact. You could impede the understanding the speaker is seeking.
- *Taking action.* Letting someone solve his own problems through reflective listening sometimes keeps the listener from taking appropriate action. For example, letting a child try to fix a bike—that is a complex task for him. Again, take caution, but don't forget the action.
- *Referring the speaker.* Sometimes in order for a problem to be solved, the speaker needs an authority figure to comment on the subject. Before the speaker will accept suggestions and referrals, he may need to build a base of trust and understanding with you, the listener.
- *Listener disclosure.* There are times in the listening process when a listener's experience can be quite helpful. Again caution is needed. This can distract a speaker and draw attention to the listener.
- *Confrontation.* Extreme caution is needed here. There are times when a speaker will show great discrepancies between what he is saying and what he is thinking or feeling. The speaker must have a great deal of trust in the listener or he will take confrontation as an attack and become defensive.

To improve your reflective listening:

- Don't fake understanding
- Don't tell the speaker you know how he feels

- Vary your responses
- Choose the most accurate feeling word
- Focus on feelings
- Develop vocal empathy
- Strive for concreteness and relevance
- Provide non-judgmental, non-dogmatic, but firm responses
- Play back the feelings that are implicit in the speaker's questions
- Reflect during brief interactions.

Use reflective listening:

- Before you take action
- Before you argue, or strongly disagree
- When the other person experiences strong emotions or wants to talk over a problem
- When the other person is speaking in code
- During a direct, mutual conversation
- When the other person wants to sort out feelings and thoughts
- When you are talking to yourself
- When you are encountering new ideas in a book, lecture or at work.

When not to listen reflectively:

- When you do not feel accepting
- When you don't trust the other person to find the solution
- When you are too close to the other person (unable to maintain a feeling of objectivity)
- When you are "hiding" by listening
- When you feel overworked, upset and depleted.

In Conclusion . . .

Much more could be said about listening. Leadership at all levels in business suffers from the lack of listening. The automobile industry didn't listen about smaller cars; steel didn't listen to the third world's progress; and no one listened to their employees. Without listening you cannot lead and participate in back-to-basics management. All communications skills are a process in which learning is ceaseless. We could say much more about the use of voice, about body gestures and other complex areas of interaction. We can only hope to give you the basics.

There are six aspects to human communication that give us problems. Being aware of them will help you add to your listening skills.

1. Words have different meanings for different people.
2. People have a tendency to code their messages and cover up the real meanings.
3. People frequently "beat around the bush" talking about one thing when something else is of greater importance to them.
4. Many people have trouble getting in touch with their true feelings and using them constructively.
5. It is easy for a listener to get distracted and lose the speaker's message.
6. We hear through our personal filters, which are developed by our own private experiences. This distorts much of what is being said.

We have discussed at great length what you must do to become an effective listener. A listener must also speak. To be a mature, balanced human being you must have both listening and speaking skills. Being a good listener can also help you become a good speaker, because you will become more fully aware of your own needs in conversation. Good listeners can often train someone with whom they are close to be a good listener.

Hints

Keys to Effective Listening

Keys to Effective Listening	Ineffective Listening	Effective Listening
1. Find areas of interest	Tunes out dry subjects	Opportunizes; asks "What's in it for me?"
2. Judge content not delivery	Tunes out if delivery is poor	Judges content and skips over delivery errors
3. Hold your fire	Tends to go into mental arguments	Doesn't make judgments until comprehension is complete
4. Be flexible	Takes intensive notes, using only one system	Takes fewer notes. Uses 4-5 different systems, depending on the speaker
5. Listen for ideas	Listens for facts	Listens for central themes
6. Work at listening	Shows no energy output; attention is faked	Works hard, exhibits active body state
7. Resist distractions	Distracted easily	Fights or avoids distractions, knows how to concentrate
8. Exercise your mind	Resists difficult expository material; seeks light, recreational material	Uses heavier material as exercise for the mind
9. Keep your mind open	Reacts to emotional words	Interprets emotional words; does not get hung up on them
10. Capitalize on fact that thought is faster than speech	Tends to daydream when listening to slow speakers	Challenges, anticipates, mentally summarizes, weighs evidence, connects material objectively to own experience, listens between the lines, reads the silent language of non-verbal communication

CHAPTER THREE
Decision Making

"A manager is a person who can make critical
judgments when the information at hand is
inferential and assumptive."
Harry Maynard

Managers who don't make decisions aren't managing—whatever their title. Nothing is more fundamental to the concept of back-to-basics management. Decision making is the fundamental activity of managers and leaders.* Even when a leader feels he doesn't have enough facts, he must act. If decisions were based only on the facts, we could feed the information into a computer and the decision would be flashed at us: a little green YES; a little red NO. But precisely because we seldom have all the facts or enough facts, human managers are necessary to make the decisions.

Whatever managerial function is being performed, whether it is training, helping plan presentations or building and maintaining morale, the manager-leader has to make judgments. His essential skill, therefore, has to be the ability to analyze, evaluate, and finally to make sound business decisions. It's a juggling act from beginning to end, and the manager-leader who is able to keep more balls in the air, control them and make them come down when and where he wants

* For leaders to be able to retain their positions they must have highly developed critical-judgment skills. They cannot delude themselves about the importance of their decisions.

them to is the one who's going to win. Who said managing was easy? It's fun and it's challenging. But easy? No! The rest of this chapter is geared toward helping you increase your ability to make decisions by honoring your "critical-judgment" skills.

"Make the Map Fit the Territory"

Many years ago, the Russian scientist Pavlov said, *"Men are apt to be much more influenced by words than by the actual facts of the surrounding reality."* The whole science of general semantics has grown up based on this key principle that says the "maps" (words) we use are never the same as the "territory" (reality). This science is very important for managers because it touches on many of the skills that make for excellence: better listening, more accurate perception, understanding behavior, more precise use of language, and other vital areas.

Let's start by defining what we mean by a "map" and a "territory."

Verbal maps: The symbols or pictures we draw mentally with the words we use.

Territory: The actual circumstance or situation we are trying to describe with our verbal maps.

Unfortunately *using* and *knowing* about words are often two different things. For example, let's just consider the word "is." Just two little letters—i and s—but "is" probably causes more problems in everyday communication than any other word in our language.

Why? Because when you say something such as . . .

it *is* good
he *is* bad
that *is* the way

you are describing something "out there" that has a certain quality of "goodness," "badness" or "be-ness." The implication is that you must agree because that which is *is*. But what we are really describing is (there goes that word again!) our feelings and our beliefs. When you talk or write about something, what you are describing are the interactions that are happening inside of you. It is only a very small part of all that is going on "out there." "Is" makes it seem that we've got hold of all reality; but what we really have is only a small piece of it. A very small piece, based mostly on a perception of what "is" is.

People deal with the real world through abstractions. We deal with reality only as we perceive, sense, and respond to things. What we really operate on is our *perceptions*. When we talk (to ourselves or to other people), we are speaking in abstractions of our perceptions.

So the words (or abstractions) are the "maps"—the "territory" is the reality out there. And no matter how hard we try, our "maps" are never, never going to be the same as the "territory."

As a manager you've got to know the territory. That's what managing is all about. Why? Because at least *70% of your day* is spent in producing or receiving verbal maps. If they are inadequate you will not be as effective as you could and should be as a manager.

Orderly, clear thinking is our ability to improve our intake of information by better listening and more accurate perception, thereby improving our processing of information (realizing assumptions and identifying information distortions). Stated simply, as information processors our task in the thinking-perceiving process is to make more critical inferences which can be turned into better premises, allowing us to make better conclusions and judgments.

Poor thinkers often make uncritical inferences, which they turn into inadequate premises, leading to erroneous conclusions and judgments.

The word adequate has been carefully chosen—a verbal map may be quite accurate and yet for your purpose be quite inadequate and misleading. . . .

An example: Two young children are in a candy store. John says to Tom. "Give me a package of gum." Tom does. When questioned by his mother, John says that Tom gave him a package of gum. His verbal map is *accurate* but it is not adequate, in that it is misleading and has nothing to do with the actual territory. John "managed" the situation; not Tom, who is presented as the culprit.

What makes a map useful is its predictability, whether they are your maps or second-hand ones (that is, maps someone else has given you). For a map to be predictable and useful, it must be accurate, adequate and must represent the territory as it is *now*. A map that represented a route last week may not show the construction work going on this week and therefore the detours that are necessary.

How do we get our verbal maps? First you should always remember that a map is not a territory. Second, you should understand that you get your verbal maps in two ways:

1. You can survey the territory yourself and make your own map.

2. You can get your map by reading or talking to other people about the territory. This is always going to be second-hand no matter how valuable.

This last point is very important. In business you must rely on other people's maps, but you should never take them for granted. Only by understanding the likes, dislikes, habits and prejudices of the people you deal with will you be able to judge the reliability of the verbal maps other people bring you. It is not a matter of trusting others, but a matter of remembering that when someone gives you a verbal map he is representing the territory as he reacted and interacted with it. Not you!

Management is the delicate balance between using the experiences of others and learning when it is important for us to survey the territory for ourselves. The proverb "One picture is worth a thousand words" is appropriate. To observe is to add predictability to your maps and plans. It is by adequately surveying the territory that scientists achieve the remarkable predictability of their verbal maps. As a manager-leader, you are constantly making decisions based on reported information. Back-to-basics management is a way of looking at reality. By using accurate, adequate and predictable maps and common sense thinking, your conclusions and decisions (those areas of critical judgment that have no black-and-white answers) will be workable with a high degree of success.

Rules of Judgmental Thinking:

1. Develop the habit of open-mindedness. Open yourself up for new ideas and new concepts. People who make the most adequate maps are those who are aware of the incompleteness of their knowledge. "Life," Samuel Butler said, "is the art of drawing sufficient conclusions from insufficient premises." As a manager-leader keep in mind the phrase "as far as I know" when you are reporting, and understand that this silent phrase should be added by you to the reports you receive. If you keep an open mind for that one hidden factor the whole course of your decision making might be changed.

2. Think in terms of degrees. We live in a fast-moving, very complicated world. Our tendency is to simplify it by speaking and thinking in terms of absolutes. Try to avoid "either/or"

type of thinking. Remember when you are making a decision, you are not making a decision against anything, all you are doing is choosing the most predictable route through the territory for that period in time.

By adding the silent phrase "up to a point," you will liberate your mind from the type of thinking that cuts down on your predictability, i.e., will my plan work? (You can't possibly know all the possibilities.) But with some predictability you can safely answer "up to a point," that is to say as far as I am able to observe and judge right now.

Caution: Watch your employees and your peers who make either/or, all/none statements. When they do, that's your hint to personally survey the territory carefully.

3. Be analytical and honest: To be able to make adequate maps, we must free ourselves from the tendency to select things that prove our point and ignore everything on the other side. Proving points by selected examples and rationalization perpetuates misinformation and nonsense.

4. Bring a little perception to your thinking: We see things not as they are, but *as we are*. The rock is large—the stew is good; when we create these kinds of verbal maps, we have a tendency to think we are talking about qualities of the rock or stew. Yet science tells us that how we taste the stew is or view the rock depends on how we are interpreting the stimuli interacting within our nervous systems. A child may see the rock as huge, while a 7-foot basketball player may view it as a rather small rock, and the stew may have no taste at all to someone with a stuffy nose. And it may have a foul taste to someone who is not accustomed to eating meat. Therefore the stew is good *to me* and the rock seems large *to me*. Science tells us the more we understand about the world the more we are sure we are dealing with the precise relationship between the *perceived* and that *perceiver*. As a back-to-basics manager this becomes extremely important to you. Do you really know the nervous systems of other people? Our reactions—as with everyone else—depend on what we are familiar with. When we say the rock is large—by adding "to me" ... "to him" ... "to her" ... "to them" ... we are making a more ade-

quate map. You are taking into account what you and others are accustomed to.

5. Watch your labels (or what a difference a difference makes): Common nouns like "house," "dog," "man," or "manager" do not tell what, when, and how—and you can't make assumptions from them. We live in a world where no two things are alike in *all* aspects. Things and ideas may be similar and, in fact, interchangeable in some instances. By adding the "what" and "how" index to our thinking (i.e. person-1 is not person-2, nor is manager-1 the same as manager-2) our thinking has the tendency to remind us to speak and think in terms of specifics. Labels are over-simplified maps that purport to be the territory. Using common labels, map judgments and stereotypes can get you into trouble and lead you to erroneous conclusions.

Caution: Watch for those who label and speak in terms of individuals, things and ideas as being identical. Possible danger! Survey the territory for the differences and hidden information.

Implementing Decisions

Up to this point we have been talking about the two functions involved in preparing to make a decision: collecting and perceiving information. Now you must make your decision, see that it is communicated properly and carried through to completion. Important: If you are not sure you have the authority to make the needed decision, the following will be helpful:

1. How far into the future will the decision affect the company? How fast can the decision be reversed? Will you be able to handle the results?
2. Does the decision affect other functions and other managers? If the answer is "yes," then you should take the information/map you have collected along with your decision on the available information and work with those to reach the decision.
3. Does the decision involve corporate values of policy? If "yes," then you must consider taking the decision to a higher authority.

4. Is the decision based on unique circumstances or one that rarely occurs? If "yes," then perhaps it should be taken further up the managerial ladder to people who may have more experience.

We are not saying that a business should be run by committee, or that only those in top position should make decisions. A decision should be made as close as possible to the function and level it affects, but care should be taken that all functions and areas that may be affected are considered. Working effectively inside the system is what makes a back-to-basics* manager. In taking a decision to a higher authority, you should give your reasoning and solution. If your solution is not accepted, it is important that you learn why it was not considered an acceptable solution. Were you misinformed or lacking some piece of knowledge? Or was there a previous decision made (without your knowledge) that affected this decision?

It is important that you teach the people working for you to make decisions. Insist your people bring you solutions, not problems. This is the only way to encourage them to think and get their creative juices flowing. What keeps people from making decisions? Perhaps the biggest inhibiting factor for most people in making decisions is risk. All decisions and solutions carry an element of risk, but by paying attention to the territory/map technique we have described this factor can be greatly reduced. There are no "little" decisions. All decisions bring changes which you must handle. All decisions deserve thoughtful consideration and your full attention while making them.

Managers-leaders make dozens of decisions everyday. Some are communicated and carried through immediately because of their nature, either one of routine or in a low-risk area. These same managers often make many other decisions which would be of great benefit to their productivity, but are never implemented.

Decisions which are not carried through usually are characterized by one or more of the following problems:

- There may not be a corporate policy which can help guide the decision maker.

* Some types of business leadership demand you deal with the system and also be able to have a greater awareness by stepping outside it in your thinking. As a leader one of your functions is to have a clearer and wider vision of circumstances than those you manage-lead.

- The previous experience of the decision maker may not be an adequate guide.
- The decision maker may not have adequate time to plan the implementation steps.
- There may be a big risk factor with unpredictable results.

The back-to-basics manager-leader does not spend time making decisions which he does not intend to carry through. It is important to remember that there is a great deal of difference between brainstorming ideas that *may* be useful and actually making the decision and seeing it through. The first may be fun—the second is managing. In companies which are highly organized there are many policies and systems set up for carrying out decisions. In some cases this leads to extensive departmentalizing; i.e., hiring personnel is left to personnel department, with the individual manager only getting the opportunity to okay the final hire. On the other hand in a strongly sales-oriented organization, the hiring of sales people may be left to the individual manager.

But all managers eventually have to make their own decisions. As a back-to-basics manager it is important that you have ready a set of processes by which you can implement decisions in a timely manner. Many decisions and solutions have a very short time span in which they are at their optimum usage, i.e. a disgruntled worker can ruin the morale of a whole department in a matter of days. Your decision on how this must be handled is needed quickly, as it can reflect directly on productivity.

In implementing decisions you should gather as much information as possible about the circumstances surrounding the decision. You must:

- Decide whom the decision will affect, i.e. personnel, other departments and managers, etc.
- Decide if you need to include other personnel in the decision and get their reactions
- Decide whom you need to communicate the decision to
- Decide whether the equipment and resources can stand the extra load that will be added
- Decide if any equipment or other resources are needed
- Decide how the decision will affect the budget or monetary situation of the corporation, i.e., purchasing new equipment, adding sales personnel, offering an additional service or part

- Decide if you need to eliminate or change any previous decision
- Decide how long will you need before the decision goes into effect
- Decide whether to delegate the planning and to whom, or to do it yourself
- Decide how you implement the decision without higher authority.

Once you have asked yourself these questions, and any others you feel are important, you are ready to begin your planning for implementation. To start your planning make a list of the following:

- All the surrounding elements of the decision needed in order for it to work; i.e., personnel, budget, goal, possible results, ways of reversing decision, equipment needed, motivation communication, presentation, etc.
- Decide which elements must be done before others can be started. Can some elements be worked on at the same time?
- The number of work hours needed to complete each element
- The name of the individual who will be responsible for seeing each aspect completed.

Look at the work hours and elements:

- Which element will take the longest time?
- Does it need any other elements to be complete?
- If "yes," add up all the time needed to finish the longest element and you will have the approximate time in which you can start to implement the decision.

Example:
Decision: Add new sales personnel
Elements:

    job description
    outlining of territory and/or client list
    set salary and commission range
    presentation to home office on decision
    presentation to sales managers and/or sales staff
    office memo on decision and/or meeting

office space
office equipment
new phone line/phone
write ad
contact employment agencies/place ad in local paper
interview time
reference check
assignment of clerical help to new staff member
training

In this list training is the last element and all others must be done before. A two-week training period will be needed. We then must estimate it will take two weeks for the employment agency or ad to bring in at least three good prospects, whom we will have to spend 1 ½ hours apiece interviewing. Reference checks may need to be done in writing and may take as long as two weeks. Therefore, we cannot have a new sales person on board and functioning for at least six weeks. The other elements we have listed should be able to be completed within a month and be ready at the beginning of training.

As a back-to-basics manager you will want to delegate most of those elements that can be done by employees (see Chapter 7 on delegation). Before you can delegate you must communicate your decision. As a back-to-basics manager-leader the phrase "people are a resource" is a working reality. Therefore much time and care must be spent in communicating and planning the results of your communication.

One of the most important skills the back-to-basics manager-leader has is the ability to communicate ideas, decisions, policies and values in such a manner that they elicit both support and motivation to a high degree.

Rule of thumb is those to whom you report should be told about your decision first. No superior likes to find out he has been left out of the communication cycle. Peers the decision will affect should be second on your list.

Communicating to Your Superior

Corporate policy and the type of decision may dictate how and what you communicate about your decisions. In communicating about a decision, even if there have been previous discussions about it, you should assume that your superior may not have remembered or be fully aware of facts and issues surrounding the decision. You must therefore plan your communication in such a manner as both to inform and elicit support.

In planning your communique, consider the following:

- What information will your superior need to feel sure that you have fully planned and considered the decision?
- Do you need to include a full written plan?
- Have you arranged your facts in a logical sequence?
- Have you stated it in language that is motivational to your superior?
- Have you included any possible negative results that everyone should be aware of?
- Have you kept it as brief as possible without excluding important facts?
- Have you provided for feedback (both positive and negative) as well as the inclusion of any further ideas that may be useful?
- Do you need to make any type of visual presentation?

If your superior does not understand your decision, *you must assume you have not communicated well or have left out important information.* Almost always this type of response is asking for further information, or for the information to be stated more clearly, etc. If you should receive a negative response or a no (without an explanation), you should assume that either you have not been aware of some vital piece of information or stated it in such a way to show the benefits. If you do not receive an explanation you should find out why the response was negative through proper channels.

Remember: Any decision which effects corporate money, hiring and firing or personnel or production at any level should be put into writing for easy file reference.

Communicating to Other Managers

Often decisions will affect other functions within a corporation, i.e., adding an additional service call may affect home office paper work, adding a reserve nut or bolt to packaging may affect inventory control, etc. Since you cannot possibly be aware of all that other managers and departments are planning, it is important that you communicate to all those who may or will be affected by your decision. Again your goal is to motivate and elicit support even if it means that another department may have to make some changes. When you communicate to other managers keep the same questions in mind as you would for your superior. This time you are looking for other managers to tell you:

- Are there areas in another department that may affect your decision?
- Will you need to include another department in your overall planning?
- Are you missing any information that can affect the outcome of the decision?
- Will you need to revamp your plan in any way?

If your planning and communication is to be effective you must know if there are places in other departments where your plan can bog down and not get the overall results you are planning to achieve. You must set up a way of checking with these departments to make sure they are completing their parts. During these preliminary stages, you should also ask other managers for suggestions on alternative methods within their divisions as a back-up course of action. The more they feel they are participating in the decisions and elements of implementation the more support you will be able to get from them. Speak and write in language that is motivational to them.

Communicating to Your Employees

We have made the statement that decisions should be made as close to the level of affected activity as possible. There are several reasons for this:

- Employees are aware of aspects of their functions and how they can best perform these functions
- Many employees (if you have hired the right personnel) can be very creative in their specific functions
- Most employees like guidelines, job descriptions and knowing how they are expected to perform, but they do not like to be dictated to or left out of decisions which will affect their work
- Employees tend to cooperate and be more supportive of decisions and systems they have had a voice in deciding.

The type of decision of course dictates where it will be made. Your job as a back-to-basics manager is to present the decision, or possible course of action, in such a manner as to both motivate them and reassure them that their best interests have been considered.

There are several methods of involving employees. The Japanese have used a system called "quality control circles," in which managers meet with a selected employee (often chosen by co-workers on a rotating basis) to discuss decisions and procedures. These employees give feedback and suggestions as well as communicate directly to their co-workers on the plans etc. This involves the employees without a large group meeting. The employees feel they are having a direct say in corporate policy and operations.

If you are to involve the employees in a general meeting to help make a decision some basic pointers are needed.

- Plan to set the meeting at a time when employees are most receptive, i.e., mid-morning on a Monday as opposed to quitting time Friday afternoon
- Instruct each member to bring pencil and paper or furnish it
- Have flip chart or blackboard at front of room; make sure that it is visible from all seats
- Have a clear statement of the goal, problem and reason for the meeting
- Prepare solutions, implementing procedures and back up research (both negative and positive) as you see it
- Plan to keep the meeting to 45 minutes.

Start meeting by:

- Presenting the reasons for the meeting
- Stating what you hope to accomplish
- Explaining the employees' part in the meeting
- Keeping to an outline of what you will cover (see section on meetings in Chapter 11, on communication skills)

  If it is a large meeting and reaching a conclusion within the meeting framework is impossible, have each employee write out his/her suggestions briefly and anonymously and hand them to you as they leave. Promise them a written report on the overall consensus of opinion.

Put the decision reached in written form, with a copy to each employee that is to be affected by it.

At this point you should ask those who will be directly affected for feedback and suggestions for implementing the procedure.

Most of your decisions must be made outside of employee input and they will have little to say about the decision itself. But those directly involved with the effects of the decisions can be asked for suggestions, and feedback concerning the implementation plans. Remember you are looking for better methods, ways to avoid trouble spots, and any information you may not be aware of that could affect the results you are after.

The type of decision will dictate whether you announce it in a meeting or through a written communique. Either way you should:

- Start by stating the goal and the reasons for the goal in motivational language to the employee (see chapter on motivation, section on motivational language)
- If you are at liberty to ask for suggestions and feedback on implementation plans, do so
- If possible ask for volunteers to carry through aspects
- When presenting the implementation plans again state in motivational language
- If the procedures are new, set as many guidelines as possible for the way you expect the functions to be carried out. At the same time do not hesitate to ask employees for feedback on how they see the task should be accomplished.
- Make sure the employees understand the deadline, ask if they have problems meeting the deadline, and how they will handle it with the rest of their work load.

Decision making is a vital function in back-to-basics management. The quality of those decisions is what will set you apart as a leader.

The techniques and ideas presented in this chapter and the rest of the book are important factors in your decision-making process. If you could see the future clearly you would know when to make changes, whom to motivate and when to listen. You would be able to make decisions clearly and with confidence. Instead, most of your day must be spent making decisions based on a little fact and lots of assumptions. The assumptive and inferential nature of managerial decisions means you must learn *how* to think rather than *what* to think. This is the thrust of decision making. Learning how to think produces the kind of quality decisions which become the cornerstone of back-to-basics management and leadership.

CHAPTER FOUR

Managing Change

"The art of progress is to preserve order amid
change and to preserve change amid order."
Alfred North Whitehead
(*Forbes*, Dec. 1, 1957)

"Preparing for the 80's" and "being prepared for the future"...
"how to avoid future shock"... all these oft-repeated phrases
underscore for anyone in management that change is the very essence
of every business. For example, we now have more people involved
with the transfer of information than we have working on assembly
lines, or in any service profession. What does this mean to you as a
manager? It means that every day your job and the jobs of those who
work under you are changing. As a back-to-basics manager, one of
your prime functions is going to be *managing change* and *leading*
others through periods of difficult change.

Employee Reaction to Change

Most people see change as a fearsome proposition; they see it as
meaning instability. Madison Avenue learned a long time ago that the
word "change" evokes fear and pain in the unconscious minds of most
people. Adjustment difficulties by people to any change (i.e., change
in routine, change in seating and working arrangements) come because
they see change as adding to the complexities of a situation rather than

reducing them. Most people change more easily when they feel *they* have been instrumental in bringing about the change, or have in some way participated in the decision that shapes the change.

This chapter is intended to help you manage change by understanding the psychology of change. We have also included a few exercises that you as a manager can use to become better adjusted to change and help those who work for and with you to do the same.

Nature of Change

Woodrow Wilson, the most scholarly of our modern presidents, said, "If you want to make enemies, try to change something." Most people dislike change. They fear change because it disrupts the way they are used to perceiving their lives. But change is unavoidable. Our whole world is constantly changing, sometimes in minor ways, such as a river gradually eroding its banks and changing both the shoreline and the flow of water.

As a back-to-basic manager-leader you must understand what happens to people's thinking when they encounter change. The brain stores each experience we have as a memory. These memories remain the same throughout our entire lives, unless we alter them in some way by adding information. We put names and labels on these memories and use them to tell us how to act and react to the circumstances we encounter.

Change occurs when we encounter circumstances or information that does not fit previous memory. When the mind encounters this opposing information the whole relationship with *that* memory is jarred. We no longer know how to act and react according to our previous experience. This leaves us with a feeling of loss and instability. This experience is painful and fearful for most people, and the fear and pain will remain until the individual has readjusted his thinking to the new experience. When we encounter change, just as with any new experience where the individual does not know what to expect, the level of anxiety rises. Consequently all individuals become anxious during change and resist it as much as possible. When discussing how an individual reacts to change, it is important to understand that even if the change is for the benefit of the individual i.e. cutting down on work load, possible increase in salary—he or she will still resist to a degree. Leadership of course demands a voluntary following. When those who are being led resist the changes implemented by the leader, the leadership loses its effectiveness. Effective leadership must manage change with the utmost care. Interestingly, Dr. Abraham Maslow (one of the first psychologists to establish guidelines of normal human behavior rather than symptoms of illnesses, and the author of many books) found that the more self-actualized a person was—the higher the self-esteem and self-confidence—the less they resisted change. In fact, in his research he found that in the human hierarchy of needs change is vital to the continuing growth of any organism. Change is a part of our nature. When we are self-confident, we are excited about change and look forward to it.

Routines and Change

Routines are addictive. And in many cases, they should be treated as addictions. They serve a definite purpose in most people's lives. They help us to avoid decisions, choices and surprises—in fact change of all kind. (NOTE: Don't confuse procedures and systems with routines. Routines help us to avoid the kind of anxieties that happen in new situations.)

In most cases routines are tyrants in both our business and personal lives. They keep us from exploring and growing. Most people have a tendency to let things happen rather than make them happen. This is one of the major problems for any manager involved in making changes.

Routines can:
1. keep productivity down
2. cause sluggishness in mental abilities
3. cause reduction of ability to observe
4. produce prejudices and biases
5. produce tunnel vision
6. produce boredom
7. produce addictions that can be harder to break than a drug habit
8. lead to a lack of adventurous spirit and the willingness to try new ideas
9. lower reaction ability
10. cause hostility and suppressed anger (leading to high levels of stress, hence the greater stress on assembly lines than at

top management levels, where one must change to remain on top).

The list could go on and on.
Caution: The more ingrained the routine, the harder it will be to implement change.

Keys to Managing Change

The first step is to start looking at your world as constantly changing . . . and become comfortable with change yourself. The more you personally explore and experience change, the more excitement you can bring to a changing situation. Once your people feel your excitement, it will be easier for them to accept change. Another critical factor for yourself and your people in managing change is *consistency*. If your attitude toward the people who work for you remains consistent (assuming it is reasonably humanistic, mature and stable), they are going to be much less resistant to any change you may need to implement.

- Set boundaries for employees and yourself and stick to them. A natural boundary will help minimize the feeling of instability and loss through a period of change (i.e. don't change job titles and seating arrangements all in the same day. Keep consistent hours.)
- Remain reliable in the eyes of your people (i.e. give them more information and explain decisions). The people who work for you—no matter how strong their egos and self-esteem—still look upon you as the authority figure. An authority figure gains reliability by explaining the whys and wherefores of a situation, not mandating them.

As a manager-leader of change you should become very aware that not only those whom you manage but many of those above you in your organization will be looking to you as a point of stability. Many businesses are lost because of:

- Changes not made that would preserve an advantage over the competition

- Poor anticipation of the reactions of employees, clients, suppliers, etc.
- Changes that in the long run are not beneficial to the corporation.

Remember: The mandate of any manager-leader is change. The viability of any enterprise or undertaking depends on its dynamics—its patterns of change and growth. The object of effective management is to create new conditions in order to maintain an advantage over the competition.

Initiating Change

A manager-leader* must start by exploring change himself. Because of our fear of change and the consequences, the best place to start is in your personal life away from the job . . . and away from your family. Start where you can have as little effect on those you must be around as possible.

Caution: Don't initiate your personal experimentation with change where unpleasant consequences might occur in either your business or personal life.

Here are some ideas for personal change:

- Take a different route to work.
- Drink a different drink than your usual one.
- Eat at a different restaurant (not when with a client).
- Try a shirt or suit of a different color.
- Change your entertainment habits.
- Change your exercise routine.

After you practice change at a personal level and become accustomed to it, start looking at the routines and habits of the people who work for you. Keep a stack of 3 x 5 cards handy. Jot down examples as you come across them. Look for those routines that can be changed with minimal consequences. During a regular meeting or office conference (don't, in the beginning, call a special meeting to initiate change of any kind; special meetings automatically raise the fear

---

* Promoted or elected leadership brings about an automatic change in an individual's life. Without preparations for the reaction to the change disaster can ensue.

level), suggest the idea of a change. Try to get your people to decide on the specific method of change. (This will drop the fear level.) Observe and note the reactions during the meeting and in the following days as the change is initiated.

When we initiate any action, we set off a series of reactions (e.g., eat more food, and you put on weight). Responses to change are directly linked to the action of change, its quality, quantity and type. You must always leave room for the psychological reaction (which is very individual in each person according to previous experiences and growth since his or her reaction to change was last observed). In order to deal with the basics of managing change you must observe all those who will or might be affected by the change. These observations will enable you to know what kinds of possible reactions might occur when you suggest changes in policies, strategies, structure, procedures, technologies and environmental areas. With these observations you will be able to do in-depth planning. For example, it takes John Doe 3 days to organize himself after a change in his sales territory. His sales drop the first week but always reach higher peaks in the next 6 months as a result of the new challenge and stimuli.

Thinking along these same lines, you should also be alert to possible reactions to changes in an employee's personal life (a newly married assistant may exhibit a drop in productivity), to changes in resources (which may cause general office confusion), changes in suppliers (slight changes in supplies can cause obstinate behavior in employees adjusting to the new product line), changes in services (change in services either offered or used can cause anger and frustration in employees), changes in customers (gaining a new or losing an old client may spread fear of the unexpected through a company), and competitive changes (new competitors can cause widespread fear in an organization).

To initiate a successful change you must take the following 6 important steps.

1. Make a critical judgment and decision. Through observation and fact finding gather as much hard information as possible, but you must still make judgments and decisions on what is not self-evident.

2. Motivate your people. Each person must see how this change will benefit him or her personally. See the next chapter on motivation.

3. Produce action. You must plan for and initiate each step for action to occur.

4. Examine possible alternatives. In your planning you must have alternatives for each major step in case of breakdowns in supplies or personnel.

5. Watch for changed behavior. The people who work for you have to change their way of relating to the work situation according to the plan. Ample time must be allowed for this step. Plans must also be made for alternative approaches if appropriate behavior is not produced within a given time.

6. Handle the consequences. You may have to fire employees or replace lost clients who cannot handle the change. In short, you have to do whatever is necessary to make the change—if it's truly needed—a viable undertaking for the corporation.

When planning a major change of any sort in a corporation or work situation prepare your people by initiating a series of small changes until everyone feels comfortable with the idea of change. Remember: Growth for you and your people lies in the unfamiliar. Only a mature person can cope successfully with the challenge of the unexplored.

Since the mandate of management is to initiate change in order to maintain a competitive edge, your next step, as an effective manager-leader, is to see where you can initiate change that will increase productivity and give you that competitive edge.

Initiating major changes is not too different from introducing smaller routine changes. Steps to take in initiating larger changes are:

- Making a decision on what to change
- Forming a written strategy involving the *what, when, where, how* and *who* of the change
- Planning for reactions to the change and possible alternative plans of action
- Planning how to motivate your people
- Getting employees involved in the method and timing of the change
- Planning which areas can remain constant in order to maintain a feeling of stability and security among your people
- Handling consequences (which, by the way, do not have to be negative). A possible influx of new business also needs to be planned for.

Employee Involvement in Change

As we stated earlier, the more the employees see themselves as helping produce and decide on the nature of change the less resistance you will encounter. Many decisions about changes in policy cannot be directly participatory, but the decisions on how and what to change can often be initiated within the staff of a corporation. (For example, the employees may not be able to help make a decision on introducing a new product line or service, but they may very well be the best source of information on how these changes could best be implemented in their individual areas of responsibility.)

Large group meetings for decision-making purposes are often very unsuccessful. There are usually a few who will resist and turn positive excitement into a series of negatives about why each idea offered would not work. When involving employees in change:

- Use as many visual aids as possible to make the change seem more real. (Most people learn 80% of what they know and understand from a visual source.)
- State the benefits in the language of motivation. (See Chapter 5 on motivation for hints in this area.)
- As much as possible, have employees solve their own problems or have at least partial solutions to any problems they bring you
- Have them write you their own individual plans for the change including implementation and ideas for alternatives, if needed
- Once each plan has been negotiated (you will most certainly need to negotiate with the employees on plans they have produced), have them rewrite and submit a final copy for your working file. (This is extremely important; research shows that written plans produce a psychological commitment from the employee and will therefore be more productive and workable.)
- Leave time in your planning for follow-up consultations in case the agreed upon plans are either unworkable or need alterations
- Add the written plans for the relevant changes to the job description of each employee position.

Your Superior and Change

Executives have lost credibility and lost positions through bad negotiations during periods of change. In major changes your superior may be relying on you as the one point of stability. Fear mounts in authority figures when they are dealing with unknown aspects of the corporation. It also develops through lack of communication. If your superior is not directly involved with your department but is showing signs of worry:

- Set up specific times and dates so that you can review the progress of the change together.
- Submit a written plan.
- Make your presentation as visual as possible.
- Use appropriate motivational language (i.e. a CEO of a public company is going to want to hear the bottom line and how this will benefit the stockholders etc.).
- Be prepared to negotiate all plans and ideas.
- Spend a great deal of time explaining the reasons for the change and how it fits in with what the corporation is aiming for.
- Ask about long-range plans and effects and how the higher-ups see the change.

Change is vital for the continuing economic growth of every company. It is those companies that plan and manage change that have a competitive edge. As a back-to-basics manager it will be your foresight and understanding of how people react to change that will allow you to manage it successfully.

Change does not have to be a fearsome proposition. As your skill increases in managing it, it will become exciting and motivating for all those concerned.

CHAPTER FIVE
Managing Motivation

"Even God himself can talk to a hungry man
only in terms of bread."
Mahatma Gandhi

We've seen it; we've heard about it; we all know about it. The mysterious life force called "motivation": the essence of leadership. The force that moves people, moves mountains, moves organizations. The impulses that can make a new world—a better world—a more productive world.

Motivation. What is it? Many things—all of them related to interpersonal relationships; all of them very, very responsive to effective leadership, to back-to-basics management, where the individual is pre-eminent and not the task.

We see motivation as an aspect of applied behavioral science—the science that studies the how and why of human interaction, either on a one-to-one basis or in groups. The behavioral scientist is interested in the same kind of things a back-to-basics manager is concerned with—how attitudes and opinions are formed (and changed); how creativity is stimulated; how motivation helps people learn and develop; how human conflict can be managed productively—and a host of other topics concerned with effective human interaction and leadership.

The point of all this research is very clear. Motivation CAN be managed. Understanding interpersonal behavior; understanding individual needs; understanding that each person is unique, although their behavior falls in consistent, recognizable patterns, are the keys to effective motivational management.

As a manager-leader, your performance will be judged on the performance and productivity of others. That is what managing is all about. One of the main goals of this book is to help you put your managerial duties in perspective. We want to motivate *you* so you'll free yourself from detail and from task-defined roles, and move on to the real challenge of leadership—managing and motivating people as individual and in groups.

Motivation Defined

Motivation is usually defined as "the drive to achieve a goal." It is primarily a mental process, a mental attitude that incites or produces a physical action leading to the accomplishment of some practical result. What gives people this drive? Why does someone want to accomplish something? Very simply . . . *to derive a benefit from the result.*

The benefit is the reward. A reward is anything that helps an individual fulfill one or more of his or her tangible or intangible needs. The reward for each individual must be as *he* or *she,* not you, defines it. The fact that you consider it a benefit doesn't make it a real benefit to the employee.

We are all motivated all the time, in that we tend to do the things we feel will be rewarding and avoid those activities that don't give us satisfaction. The problem is that, being as complex as we are, human beings rarely agree on what is "rewarding" and what is not. So the job of the manager is to make the fit—to help the employee feel that the goals of the group, the department, the organization, are the same (or parallel) to his or her own personal goals. That, perhaps more than anything else, is the art of the effective, back-to-basics manager.

An employee's job behavior is always motivated by the benefits he or she seeks. Thus you already have the motivation mechanism in place in every individual. Find out what his or her needs are, convert them into benefits and you get motivation. As a back-to-basics manager you should analyze your employee's behavior as a function of his or her desire to fulfill two types of needs and meet two types of goals:

Tangible needs: The substantive payoffs the person doing the job wants from the job

Intangible needs: The reasons *why* people want the rewards they do from their jobs; achievement, belonging, security, ego

Business job goals: Fairly specific goals, usually measurable and dealing with objective matters

Behavioral job goals: Less easily measured, dealing with changes in behavior or interpersonal skills that will help achieve a business job goal

As complex as humans are, the theory of behavior modification and motivation can be boiled down to a formula. It is a four-part process as follows:

$$G + N + R = PP$$

G = goal (business or behavioral)

N = needs (tangible and intangible)

R = rewards (what's in it for me?)

PP = productive performance (performance that is highly motivated, enthusiastic, effortful, determined, vigorous, sustained and productive)

Linking work goals (G) with needs (N) leads to rewards (R). This produces commitment—the desire to achieve the goal that leads to highly motivated and productive performance (PP).

To bring this into focus, we need to spend some time discussing intangible and tangible needs.

Tangible and Intangible Needs and Motivation

In the 50's, Dr. Abraham Maslow defined and listed human needs in a hierarchy that for the first time identified some of the *whys* in human achievement and motivation. In managing motivation this list of needs is used today throughout industry and business.

Maslow's hierachy of needs appears in chart form on the facing page. Generally speaking, healthy emotional people have the tendency to make a natural progression, starting at the bottom and working their way up. However, it is common to find healthy individuals in a variety of degrees in several levels at one time. This is why you will find your people in various levels and various degrees of several levels.

How do you as a back-to-basics manager identify what needs your people have?

Chart I

START AT THE BOTTOM AND WORK UP

INTANGIBLE NEEDS	DEFINITION	WHAT CAN HAPPEN IF NEED IS NOT FULFILLED
6. Self-realization	Need to develop feelings of growth, learning, maturity, increase in competency, mastery over situations	Feelings of futility, alienation, bitterness
5. Independence	Need for privacy, need not to be manipulated, need to show responsiblity, need for opportunity to control one's life	Feelings of frustration, entrapment, exploitation, despair
4. Esteem	Need for recognition, status, prestige, approval, self-respect	Low self-image, self-doubt, loss of confidence
3. Social	Need for companionship, belonging, affection, acceptance	Loneliness, boredom, feelings of being unlovable and unloved, low self-image
2. Security	Need for stability, predictability, safety	Tension, anxiety, fear, panic, uneasiness
1. Biological	Bodily requirements for healthy living	Pain, illness, physical discomfort, impairment, etc.

1. Observe their behavior.
2. Link their tangible needs to intangible needs. For example, an individual says he wants to belong to a company with low turnover. This means he is seeking security, and his benefit will be in the area of security.

Caution: People do not reveal their tangible wants and needs unless they are asked. You must probe to find out their wants and desires. We have compiled a list of attributes that fall under each of the categories of needs that will help you identify some of the underlying desires of your people. Study it carefully.

How to Identify Intangible Needs

Security need signs	*Individual behavior*
Cautiousness; neutrality; procrastination; follows the leader; prefers solitude; overly strong respect for tradition; pessimism; dependence	Self-protective; doesn't get involved in disputes; puts off projects with high stakes; quiet; restrained in attitude; does best in structured situations; strong believer in routines and status quo; saves for a rainy day; lets others carry the ball; does not show leadership drives
Social need signs	*Individual behavior*
Amiability; agreeability; strives for acceptance; extreme loyalty; impatience with structure; gregariousness; sensitivity to others; tendency to color facts; indecisiveness	Very friendly; outgoing attitude; makes others feel at home; voices agreement; does not take unpopular stand; has trouble sticking to task or topic in conversation; may pay undeserved compliments; dedicated team player; bored by details; plays it by ear; exaggerates; makes delays or changes mind frequently on decisions

Esteem need signs	*Individual behavior*
Boastfulness; domination; positiveness; opinionated; values status; rarely credits others; preference for influential people; strong desire to win	Overstates achievement; in conversation stresses "I & Me"; monopolizes conversation; puts others down; shows skill at building his or her own image; holds dogmatic views; speaks in terms of absolutes; talks a lot about getting ahead; rarely praises others; is extremely competitive; does little socializing with peers; spends time with "higher-ups"; rarely blames himself for not achieving goals

Independence need signs	*Individual behavior*
If seeking independence— argumentative; rugged individuality; shows resistance to others' ideas; takes fixed positions; bids for autonomy; attempts to control; shows self-confidence; *or* if individual feels he or she has gained independence—demonstrates collaboration; acceptance of help; full disclosure; openness to ideas	Argues minor points; shows belligerence; dislikes supervision; criticizes others' ideas; is sarcastic and stubborn; doesn't like working on team; wants to lead those groups or "be in control"; *or* is self-assured; doesn't brag; works willingly with others; will accept help or further training; will present all sides of a story; is receptive to new ideas; curious and eager to learn

Self-realization need signs	*Individual behavior*
Probing; candid; task-oriented; seeks challenge; risk-taking; shows preference for the new; ability to confront difficult situations; need to share ideas; sensitivity to others' ideas	Curious; eager to learn; probing; Socratic questioning abilities; very direct, frank, honest in appraisals; can give and receive legitimate criticism; highly creative in whatever endeavor;

long attention span; dislikes
details not directly related to
projects; constantly seeks to
challenge self and knowledge in
order to grow; wants to try what
no one else has done; enjoys
elements of risk; takes
calculated chances; shows
tendency to teach and share
knowledge; sound philosophical
base; holds intelligent
conversations; logical; willingly
arbitrates situations of conflict;
tends to emanate strong personal
magnetism; does not use
knowledge as weapon; good
communication skills; expert at
listening and hearing what the
other person is trying to say;
well-developed democratic
personality; need for private
time to study and develop self;
good at group dynamics
situations

The intangible needs always manifest themselves in the ways individuals and peers interact in interpersonal relationships. You will have to spend time observing your employees and talking to them to link the intangible with the tangible desires. It is important to note that as levels of intangible needs are met and satisfied within the individual, a natural progression will take place to the next level of growth. This is why you will often see a person who has been highly motivated and doing a good job suddenly become discontented. He or she is now ready to move to the next level, and this is a sign that his or her concept of an appropriate benefit is changing. A performance appraisal conversation thus becomes important about every 6 months to keep a clear picture of each individual's changing motivational needs. To be able to motivate employees you must be able to meet either their tangible or intangible desires and needs. Tangible needs are often in short supply (bonuses, promotions, pay raises, etc.) and cannot be met. It is important to transform these stated tangible desires and needs into intangible terms. Once you have understood the unspoken intangible need you will be able to proceed in achieving a high level of motivation in your employees.

Examples of Tangible Needs Transformed to Intangible:

Individual's tangible desire	*Possible intangible need*
"I want to be considered for a management position."	Esteem needs and perhaps some independence needs. Can you change his or her working structure so part of these needs are met? A good candidate for transferring some of your more tedious work to show him or her some of the aspects of being a manager.
"I would like a tougher assignment to tackle; I need more challenge."	Self-realization needs with possible esteem needs. This person has good leadership possibilities and is a prime candidate for special projects. He or she will also benefit from training others, etc.
"It bothers me that we have had so much turnover this year."	Security needs; putting this person in a very structured situation will help motivation. Also, letting him or her know what the job entails *exactly* each time you give an assignment will be very motivational.
"I would like more variety in what I am doing."	Possible social needs and self-realization. Individual will be motivated by being allowed to help form some kind of group effort, e.g., office softball team, social gathering at end of quarter for payoff in office for meeting or surpassing quotas.

These are only a few examples of how meeting people's varying desires can be used to promote business objectives. You may have to analyze conversations to identify their needs and desires. Combining conversation and observation will give you the clues you need. The motivation will depend on how creative you can be in thinking of ways to use the information you have gathered.

Remember: Understanding the benefit—"What's in it for me"— motivates all individuals. It produces the commitment and drive needed to achieve the job goal. People work with commitment when they have a personal reason to do so. The job goal becomes something they really want to achieve.

Other People Needs

We have been dealing with people's needs which are interactional only at a social or work level. This does not mean these are their only needs. Other needs frequently manifest themselves in non-interactional performance. These include intellectual needs, aesthetic needs, the need to gratify curiosity, the need to know.

These needs are not basic to behavior on the job. But they do influence the behavior and desires of employees. The more you understand all of the needs of all of your people, the easier it will be to motivate them.

Language of Motivation

One source of motivational problems is the language in which management speaks*—the language of profit and loss. But individual behavior is benefit-seeking behavior and is not related to profit unless it answers the unspoken question "What's in it for me?" Therefore, speaking in profit and loss language "turns off" many employees.

The language of management includes such ideas and words as "planning," "organizing," "integrating," "measuring," "bottomline" . . . etc. This is language that as a back-to-basics manager you must think in and plan in . . . but you must always remember that it is not the language to speak in when you're trying to motivate human beings.

*Successful leaders seem intrinsically to know how to speak to their followers to bring about motivation.

Here's an example of management language: A manager presents a new plan; he talks of what the plan is supposed to do and presents the whole picture; he speaks of the organization; how each member will be integrated into the new system and how it will be able to monitor performance; and what bottom-line results are expected. His audience, however, is listening for the language of motivation . . . for words such as "participation," "opportunity," "benefits and rewards," "involvement," "meaningfulness." If these are not heard, it may be assumed that their well being has been left out. The manager has been speaking in terms of the company and the individual person wants and needs to hear about benefits if the plan or idea is to be effectively carried out.

The conclusion is obvious. When you present ideas, think in terms of *benefits* and what the intangible needs of your people are. There are approximately 4 billion people in the world and 4 billion "languages." If you are to be effective as a back-to-basics manager, you must constantly change how you speak in order to reach your audience. The language in which you speak to your people should focus on the benefits and satisfy the need to belong, to be recognized, and to have emotional and economic security. If you speak in this language, you will have a highly motivated team.

Motivational Timing

One of the main obstacles to motivation is the inability to create a two-(or more) way dialogue. In order to communicate and speak the language of motivation, both you and your staff must have a "readiness to participate." Communication is never one way. Receptivity is the key word in timing. Are your people ready? Are you?

Receptivity is the willingness to take in (receive) what the other person knows, believes, thinks and feels. It is the willingness to pay attention, concentrate, weigh, evaluate; to give the other person a chance to get through. It is a willingness to cooperate in the communication process.

To receive is to acquire (take in) and to meet with. (A receptive communicator actively works at meeting the other person's mind so understanding can take place.) It is a *collaboration* between two or more people.

When you have receptivity and receiving together, you have a condition of high receptivity.

Why is all of this important in motivation and timing of motivation? Because, no matter how well you have observed, listened, defined and are able to speak in the language of motivation, if the person you are talking to—and you—are not receptive at a high level . . . no motivation, no action will take place. Like everything else, receptivity is a matter of degree. You can't have a curve of participation with just high and low and no middle. The optimum is high but this is not always possible. What is the right time to motivate? This depends on whether the individual is in a high mode of receptivity or a low one. A low mode is not going to produce much motivation. You must be able to judge what state each person is in.

Signs of Low Receptivity Behavior:

Individual is argumentative, challenges ideas, makes flatly negative assertions, makes statements that are absolute and unqualified, interrupts, is impatient, inattentive, defiant, fidgety, or intentionally rude. Or you may have someone who is silent, apathetic, nervous or gives you unquestioning compliance, is overagreeable or asks harmless questions that have little or no relevance to the subject. Caution: What we have described above is characteristic of a direct rejection of ideas and of the entire communication process. Indirect rejection is harder to spot and will come from those with greater security and social needs.

Signs of High Receptivity Behavior:

Qualified responses, e.g., "I'm not sure I buy that" as a compared to the flat assertion "You are absolutely wrong"; approval which comes after questioning and conversation interaction and is less exuberant than overagreement; a tone of deliberate and thoughtful communication, involvement and debate; a willingness to give and take and arbitrate differences; questions that are pointed and appropriate to the business at hand; openly expressed doubts (not flat assertions); requests for more clarification on topics; good open body language (e.g., hand gestures that say "receptivity," not "stop," arms not crossed over chest, relaxed leaning forward positions etc.).

How to Use the Signs

If during the conversation the individual continues to tighten and show decreasing receptivity, *discontinue the conversation.* Prolonging it may set up a pattern for later rejection. If there seems to be a loosening up, continue the conversation.

Caution: Give both yourself and the individual time to loosen up. You should feel each other out before beginning the conversation in earnest.

"Get-The-Best-Out-Of-Them" Management

The back-to-basics manager-leader uses the kinds of motivational practices we have been speaking of, gets his or her people involved strategically with decisions, delegates in a planned, purposeful way, ties people's needs to company goals and quotas, encourages analysis and criticism of what's going on and practices *two-way* motivational communication. He or she motivates through understanding, involvement and commitment.

It is almost a step-by-step process. It starts with getting into the mind of the employee and understanding the insights, agreements or disagreements that flash by as you talk. It goes something like this:

1. Can I do this job?
2. Can I achieve the level of performance being asked of me?
3. What will performing well do for me?
4. How valuable or durable are the outcomes I expect to get from high or low performance?

All of this is a flash as you discuss one simple assignment! But this is what goes on in the mind. With this kind of understanding, the manager will find that he has and can produce high creativity, low-to-average turnover, optimal growth, resolution of disagreements and an open, involved, goal-oriented environment in his or her team. The end result will be a constantly high output.

CHAPTER SIX

Managing Time

> "You can only manage time in those moments
> when you are alert to what is going on within
> you and around you."
> James T. McCay

The analogy of the difference between the time spent in the dentist's chair and the time spent in pleasure is a common one, depicting the idea of time as relative.

No one has ever really been able to define the psychological function of time in the mind. But, we can talk about some of the attributes of leaders and back-to-basic managers who seem to have a better grasp of what time really is and how to use it. Nothing is more important to the back-to-basics manager-leader than the ability to manage time and to use it profitably. Leaders in both the private and public sectors of our country have always had a different sense of time than other employees or the average person on the street. What others may label "dedication" may simply be a different sense of time. Back-to-basics managers do not orient themselves by the usual "time for lunch," "time for dinner" but by a different kind of time awareness that relates more directly to situations and circumstances. For them, time has a direct relationship with productivity. They do not vent their frustrations by constantly complaining there is not enough time. Instead, they direct their interest towards the use of time and the quality of the time spent. The vast amount of material written about time management treats time in a purely mechanical way—adding 10 minutes here, subtracting

30 minutes there, etc., etc. Very little is said about the *quality* of time. The effective back-to-basics manager and the successful leader know better. He realizes that time, like motivation, has very little to do with *things*. The way he sees it is very clear, precise and action-oriented. Time, according to our back-to-basics definition, is not seconds and minutes but our attitude towards our actions in any finite time period.

No one can change the quantity of time you have to work with. You can only increase the quality of time. This deals directly with attitudes; how *you* see time, how it relates to you, your job, and the people you lead. Your job as a manager is not just to make better use of *your* time, but to learn how to help the people who report to you manage time better.

Breaking the Time Barrier

Every moment of our day, millions of signals from all of our senses (eye, ear, nose, taste, touch) are being sent to our brains. There the signals are sorted out and we get impressions in forms of thought. These thoughts first appear as symbolic mind pictures before they are translated into thinking terms (words). These thoughts control our actions and reactions to situations . . . and our use of time. If you have no picture, you have no action. If the picture in your mind is fuzzy or confused, you will feel fuzzy and hesitate before acting. You can't act without mind pictures. Only when we have a clear picture of a situation are we willing to act quickly, definitely, and efficiently—with *full force* and *full energy*. The speed with which you make pictures governs the swiftness of your actions.

You can increase your output as you increase your ability to get clear, accurate and fast impressions of what is going on around you. That's a learned skill. The three steps that will speed up this process are:

- Increasing your available energy,
- Increasing your alertness,
- Increasing your knowledge and experience.

The Power of Available Energy

The relationship of energy with time is very direct. Lack of energy decreases productivity and decision-making abilities. Both the mind and body go into slow motion. Simple tasks become draining, and the relationship between facts and acts does not seem clear to the individual. The more energy the individual brings to the problem, the clearer the picture, the swifter the mental reaction, and the faster he can go into action. The back-to-basics manager and leader always has more available energy to apply and use. Have you ever noticed that people who get a lot done, and seem to be full of energy, are always thought of as postitive? Conversely, those people who have little energy and get little done, are thought of as negative. We know something is wrong . . . and we know productivity will be affected. Negativity and pessimism use great amounts of our energy whether it is a negative emotion, a negative outlook or defensive behavior. The next time you are at a meeting where the energy is flowing, note what happens to eveyone's energy when someone turns pessimistic and negative. The same thing applies with feelings of anxiety, fear, doubt, uncertainty. When energy drops, our actions have a tendency to slow down.* We lose our concentration and our ability to focus our attention. This, in turn, has a profound effect on the *quality* of our time usage. Most people have several facets to their personalities. Whenever that facet that has fears, doubts and is anxious comes into play, energy and attention automatically drop. In fact, if you pay attention you will find that one of the prime distractions is an inner dialogue going on between an upbeat approach and doubts and fears. The more you cut down on these "battles," the more attention and energy you will have available for use.

When you become aware of this kind of dialogue going on in your mind, simply turn your attention to something else, i.e. think of something for a moment that gives you great pleasure, or put your full attention to the conversation going on around you. Get your mind off the negatives.

Learn to read your own body language. If you are tense and under stress, you won't be functioning well and you won't be producing. You can do something about it. The back-to-basics managers and leaders shield energy by:

- Ridding themselves of negative emotions
- Ridding themselves of unnecessary inner dialogues that keep them preoccupied

*Leaders are often still going strong when their employees have to rest. Biographical information on many leaders and creative people often show these successful people seem to understand the use of their energy in relationship to time to an extraordinary extent.

- Learning to relax
- Allowing plenty of time for rest
- Learning to change their activities so they can change the course their energy takes
- Doing physical exercises to increase their energy
- Learning to turn off the flow of negative energy in meetings and one-on-one contacts.

The Power of Alertness

Lack of concentration or alertness is probably the greatest single factor in reducing your output and affecting your use of time. In studying leaders and back-to-basics managers who have achieved great success, the single most important factor was the element of undivided attention or single-mindedness.

Trying to concentrate on more than one idea, or listening to several ideas at once, will divide your attention. Hence . . . loss of power and energy output. Examples: Trying to remember a board meeting in detail takes your total attention because all of your attention must go to form a mental picture. If you try to remember a phone call and observe a new employee at the same time, your pictures become fuzzy. The struggle uses up not only your alertness, but energy and time as well.

Remember: Any time you are preoccupied, and not giving your full attention to what is going on, you are not free to manage your time and are working at less than your available energy output.

Anytime we habitually do things (walk through offices, attend meetings, conduct conversations) we are on "automatic control" and not functioning at our full capacity. We are preoccupied. Our attention is divided. The back-to-basics manager is aware that all actions have a direct relation to productivity. One of his prime goals is to train himself to keep his mind at the peak of awareness and alertness.

Routines and habits are deadly to this peak awareness, as are attitudes of doing it by the book. By doing things automatically we overlook small signals and warnings, as well as new opportunities. Alertness and increased energy output demand changing routines and habits. Every time you change a routine you must become more alert in order to handle it in a new way. To increase your alertness and awareness, your mind must be stretched and activated in ways it is not used to.

The following are some suggestions for increasing alertness:

- Change routines
- Give yourself a new challenge that must be worked at each day
- Learn a new skill (playing a musical instrument, a new sport, new language)
- Learn to notice when you are acting in a robot fashion rather than paying attention
- Learn to take 3 minutes of uninterrupted time *every hour,* during which your mind has time to daydream and refresh itself
- Take time each night to review your day from beginning to end in mind pictures. This will help you spot those times when you were not alert.

When we are preoccupied, great chunks of our time pass without our noticing them go by. This is why we are surprised that a movie has been two hours long (one we have enjoyed) while being in a dentist's chair for half an hour (where we are at full attention) seems an eternity. When the back-to-basics manager is at attention, alert-time is psychologically expanded.

Daydreaming and preoccupation are important parts of our mind functioning. They let our minds recoup and restore themselves, and they let new ideas and desires be known . . . but uncontrolled and unplanned daydreaming and preoccupations leave an undisciplined mind which inevitably leads to less freedom in managing your time efficiently and effectively.

The Power of Knowledge and Experience

In order for today's leaders to lead intelligently, they must be constantly learning and dealing with new information. They cannot rest on past experience and knowledge for many decisions and solutions will have to be outside previous experience. This third way of increasing our impression-making abilities, and therefore our freedom to manage time, is through gaining knowledge and experience. Why is knowledge and experience necessary? Because . . .

- What we see and receive as impressions is mostly directed by what we *expect*

• Our previous experiences are constantly shaping our present experiences and attitudes.

This means that without new knowledge and fresh experiences, we remain in a rut. What we are seeing when we are alert is being limited. Seeing and experiencing new ideas is somewhat difficult and painful to our brains. It means forming new categories, new connections and new ways of seeing. That's a challenge, but sometimes it can be very scary.

When a blind person is first given sight, his experience is a painful one. Not from the light, but because his knowledge was based on a different way of "seeing," and he is not familiar with seeing in this new way. No matter how wonderful, it's a painful readjustment. In order to gain new knowledge and experience you must learn to see in a new way. You are used to seeing the way you have learned to form your present perceptions. New knowledge demands changed perceptions.

As your experience in any area grows, you can "see" more in that area. Only through persistence and self-discipline will you gain *insight, knowledge* and the ability to handle time more effectively.

Breaking the Time Barrier

There are two ways management has traditionally used to increase time efficiency: (1) Through methods of selectivity and priorities and (2) through methods of delegation and elimination. The big problem occurs after you have selected tasks and decided on priorities that are a "must"; then delegated all that can be delegated . . . and you *still* don't have enough time to be productive. Today's back-to-basics managers and leaders must understand the principle of *refinement* as related to output. As we increase our capacity to discriminate and refine our tasks, we can increase our output.

Increasing Your Time Management Skills

Most opportunities for increasing your time management skills will occur in your everyday work situation. As you increase your alertness and energy output, you will be able to define more readily those areas which need improvement. Time management skills are surrounded by areas of "knowing."* What we mean by this, is those who are efficient time managers know:

- When to start a project
- When to stop
- How to set priorities
- How to delegate
- How to communicate ideas effectively so time is not wasted
- How to say *no*
- How to handle interruptions (so they are not the main thrust of the day)
- How to use problem solving techniques effectively
- How to give appropriate time, effort and attention to different projects and ideas
- How to manage change
- How to take time off
- How to manage their personal-decision time
- What their personal best working time is
- When to be creative
- How to make a time plan.

Time Plans and Where to Start

You start making your time plan by analyzing how and where you spend your time.

- Make out a list of your daily activities (from the time you get up in the morning)
- Put an approximation by each item of how much time you spend
- For one week, keep track of the time actually spent
- Identify those areas which are taken up by preoccupation
- Identify those areas where delegation would free your time
- Make a daily and weekly priority list of (1) must do, (2) should do, (3) would like to do
- Set aside 10 minutes every two hours to go over your priorities, crossing off those done, and making new additions (decide if these priorities can be moved into less urgent categories)

* Leaders are surrounded by a mystique that often comes from this "knowing." Followers are often mesmerized by this quality in very charismatic leaders.

- Put recreation or exercise time into your daily and weekly schedule (do not include the weekend)
- Set aside development time to work on specific managerial skills
- Set aside a 10-minute period every day (without interruptions) where you honestly evaluate your progress. Decide then where you need to concentrate your efforts
- Keep refining and practicing your skills. Make time your ally instead of your enemy.

Time Management Myths

One of the most common problems for people having trouble with time management is that they believe the myths that have grown up about the subject. Some of the most common are:

- *Managers who are the most active get the most done.* Many people tend to confuse activity with results. Employees and managers who are the most insecure often work at levels inversely proportional to the certainty of direction and confidence of results. Activity becomes an end in itself.
- *The most efficient manager is the most effective.* Unfortunately this does not hold. To be efficient on the wrong project or efficient on the right project at the wrong time, may be highly ineffective. Doing the right things right is both effective and efficient. It's not the minutes and hours but what you do with them.
- *The harder one works, the more one gets done.* Experience has proven over and over again that every hour spent in effective planning can save 3-4 hours in execution and insure better results. *Work smarter, not harder*
- *An open door policy improves a manager's effectiveness with people.* Effective managers agree on an imperative need for planned unavailability. The "always available" manager finds it impossible to plan, work with priorities and set goals and objectives. On a very deep level he may welcome interruptions as a way of avoiding problems only he can solve
- *Identifying problems is the easy part of problem solving.* Much time and effort are spent solving the wrong problems. By failure to ascertain the real problem, managers inevitably waste time

The Quality of Time

The important question is: "Time for what?" You can organize yourself, learn to read faster, cut down on phone calls, interpersonal relations and lunches. That's the easy part. The hard part is knowing what to do with your time. Developing goals, stepping back to reflect on what's going on around you. A little quiet time every day to recharge your batteries is essential. You're a manager. Time is your ally, your helper, your employee. Make it work for you.

CHAPTER SEVEN
Managing Delegation

"Proper delegation is an indication of a
manager's trust and faith in his people."
James F. Evered

Every organization is full of people who "live" their jobs—hurrying
and scurrying, no time for lunch, no time to talk—then back home
packing a bulging briefcase—day after day, week after week, month
after month. Should we be impressed? Or puzzled? Does this greater
personal involvement suggest an effective management style or does it
pinpoint a serious flaw in the manager's ability to delegate?*

Studies have revealed some very interesting psychological problems
concerning delegation. When asked to define "delegation," most
managers had no problem (even though they might be having problems
delegating). The problems seemed to have very little to do with the act
itself. Most delegation problems occur because of the feelings and
emotions of those who are delegating.

The problems of delegation will be easier to understand if we first
understand what the art of delegation is. Delegation is the art (and the

---

* Rensis Likert's investigations into leadership and management showed successful
leaders, in time of crisis and heavy workload, sustained their leadership roles. They
delegated tasks and were available to handle management problems as they arose.
They did not roll up their sleeves and do the work themselves.

discipline) of handing someone else a job that you can do perfectly well, and probably better than, the person to whom you are giving the job. Delegation deals with the absolute necessity of decentralizing every managerial job. Most matters which cross a manager's desk usually can be put into one of three different categories. These are: (1) those involved with routine or repetitive tasks, (2) those involved with short-range emergencies, and (3) those which involve long-range planning and implications. An intelligent and able manager and leader can quickly set up a system for category 1, which leaves adequate provision for category 2, and even more time for his most challenging tasks in category 3, which, when concluded, should also be delegated.

The lunch-snatcher, the briefcase lugger and the detail-hugger all probably suffer psychologically from the loss of control which is part and parcel of the delegation process.** When they give away a piece of work it automatically brings about feelings that can be expressed as: (1) power loss, (2) authority loss, (3) a certain degree of loss of meaning, (4) constraint and restraint, (5) loss of achievement from doing a job that he knows he can do well.

Unfortunately, being aware of these feelings does not mean they won't get in the way. The will to succeed as a manager must be great enough to deal with them. If it isn't, there will always be problems in delegating. One of the myths about leadership and management, which creates confusion in a work place, is "to be effective you must be able to handle each task youself." Leadership skills and back-to-basics management are not technique oriented but require skills in directing and supervising. A manager does not need to know *how* a word processor works. He must understand *what* it does and how to delegate tasks to those who do understand the *how*. Leadership must be able to retain an objective overview of the work situation. This means that to function at his best the leader must not be emotionally or physically involved with the work (this does not mean he is not empathetic to those doing the tasks). The emotional as well as physical involvement of a leader will often lead to subjective view points which hinder decision-making ability and effective supervision.

**Managers who do not delegate well often tell you they have little or no time for such tasks as performance appraisals, motivation, long- and short-term planning, etc. Back-to-basics manager-leaders know that these types of functions must be a priority for a productive work situation, which means they must delegate every task possible.

Anytime we hand over a job, we are going to feel some sense of loss. We are losing something that was important and gratifying to us, or we would not have learned how to do it well. For example:

- A feeling of power loss occurs because, to a large extent, our sense of personal power comes from what we know and what we have achieved.
- Authority loss occurs when we risk letting someone else become as much of an authority on a subject as we ourselves are. What we feel is a loss of control.
- Meaning loss occurs when we lose track of those things which give our life meaning. We feel a loss of direction and purpose when this happens.
- We feel a loss of personal expression when we delegate. To help others learn, we must let them do it their way, not our way.
- We feel a loss of achievement when we no longer are doing the things that we do well. (Even those chores of a very routine kind.) We no longer have that good feeling of accomplishment and completion.

Caution: None of these feelings should be considered negative. They are very normal and very common. Being aware of what they are will help you deal with them more effectively—and help you delegate tasks more effectively.

Mastering the art of delegation, like the mastery of any art form, demands patience and earnest effort. But it's of prime importance if you are to succeed as a back-to-basics manager. Your job is to think, plan and supervise as much as possible. In practicing the art of delegation you are: (1) freeing yourself from tasks that can be done by someone else, (2) concentrating your available energy on that which no one else can do better or be responsible for, (3) giving those under you a chance to develop and learn how to carry more of the load, (4) freeing time available for the development of your leadership abilities and thinking of innovative ideas which will keep your company ahead of the competition, (5) freeing your thinking from details which may keep you from obtaining an overview of the work situation you are managing, (6) finding out who can be trusted to carry out tasks. (This will be very useful in making both plans and decisions.)

Delegation is a five-step process. Each one of the steps must be followed for it to be successful. It will be easier to master the steps of the process if you will review any delegation you are doing at present to see if you have included all the steps, and which steps need improving.

If you have not been using all of the steps that are included in the successful delegation process, start in small areas, then work up to the more sophisticated and complicated areas.

The steps in the delegation process:

- *Policy must be stated clearly and explicitly.* This means you must have a clear picture in your mind of what company policy is and what your division or department policies are. Relevant policies must be transmitted each time you delegate a job.
- *Tasks must be defined.* This means that your people must have a clear picture of both your job and their jobs. Job definition gives you the authority to delegate and the individual the understanding of how the specific job fits into his or her personal job description.
- *Goals must be set.* When you set goals you give a sense of direction. You also let people know how they are doing. Goals must be set for each job delegated and transmitted. On larger jobs you will want to include the individual's ideas on time limits and the methods to be used in achieving the task. The back-to-basics manager and leader also speaks of the task or assignment in benefit language to the employee, i.e., participation, job growth.
- *Ideas must be communicated.* This means for the task you have delegated to be successfully completed you must have meaningful two-way conversations: (1) The person you are delegating to must show you he or she understands the task. (2) He should tell you about any hesitations he has. (3) He should have a chance to add his ideas and methods. (4) You should be sure you have motivated him according to his benefit needs.

  Delegating effectively also means that you, the manager, have had meaningful communication with your supervisor, using his knowledge and experience to suggest ideas on how the job can best be accomplished.
- *Controls must be established.* You can delegate a task, but not the responsibility that it gets done. Therefore you must have a way of knowing if the job is done, or if not, to step in and take action. You can't delegate without control. As a manager you

must develop a system of checks and balances to keep in contact with jobs being done.

Some "Do's" and "Don't's" On Delegating Authority

When you delegate authority, you are giving the individual the right to do it his way. You will dampen his enthusiasm and feelings of accomplishment if you insist that it be done only your way. For example, if you give your secretary the authority to answer repetitive inquiries—by letter, or memos for your signature perhaps—when the letter or memo comes across your desk, *don't change it.* As long as the substance is correct, what matter does it make if the style is not yours? It can be a real growth experience for the person involved.

Planning Delegation

Saying you need to delegate more is easy. But planning and deciding on what should be delegated becomes more difficult. As a rule of thumb those tasks which you do well and can train someone else to do should be considered. The first part of planning should be to list tasks that can be delegated. Here's how to go about it:

- List all the tasks you are responsible for
- Keep a running list of all you do during the day for two weeks. (Even answering the phone during lunch break.)
- Keep a time sheet or estimate the time needed for each task
- Make a list of the qualities and/or skills needed for each task
- Review your personnel and their skills and attributes
- Place the name of a staff member by each task matching skills and attributes with the need of each task
- Make a list of all the details and instructions an employee will need to accomplish each task
- Decide on check points and balances for each task
- Decide on alternative time plans for each task (in case the job needs to be redone or is not finished)
- Review in your mind all tasks that you have previously delegated. Examine the causes of failures as well as successes.

If you are not used to delegating or have been delegating very little pick two assignments that would cause the least amount of upset (and time, on your part) if they are not finished or need to be redone.

Successful Attributes of Delegation

The back-to-basics manager and leader

- Avoids trespassing on authority once it is given
- Periodically checks performance
- Encourages his people to make decisions
- Defines jobs for his people so they are provided with the greatest challenge and opportunity
- Inspires his people with the will to work towards objectives and goals
- Makes full use of the skills and abilities of his people
- Has his people participate in setting work objectives and schedules
- Gets group reaction before going ahead with projects
- Generates a sense of belonging
- Encourages cooperation with others
- Goes to bat for his people.

Delegation Review

Not every task that is delegated gets done or is done correctly. When reviewing a poorly or unfinished task that has been delegated, make sure all the steps have been included. One of the biggest problems in communicating a task that is to be delegated is our intimate awareness of the task, which is not usually shared by subordinates. Thus, much usable knowledge and information that should be passed on with the assignment often is not. This breakdown in communication can be avoided by:

- Addressing the task as if you know nothing about it so you include all the steps no matter how obvious
- Making sure you give a full set of instructions including warnings about unseen pitfalls
- Seeking feedback, i.e. having the employee repeat his understanding of the task and all the elements in *his own words;* you may then see if he does understand the task and directions
- Getting the employee involved, asking for any suggestions he may have on accomplishing the task—or how he feels he can best do it

- When delegating a task for the first time, having check points set up so major problems can be avoided.

Setting Up Checks and Balances

Checks and balances in delegation allows you to retain control. Since ultimately you are the one responsible for the work, you must have ways of seeing that work is done according to your instructions and standards. The system that you develop needs to let you know: (1) If the task was done; (2) What the results of the task are; (3) If any complications or problems occur; (4) What are any short- or long-range effects on business; (5) If any new ideas or ways of proceeding have been developed; (6) Whether the employee feels he can handle a similar task again.

Not every task needs a verbal discussion. Nor do employees need to be praised or criticized in person for their performance on every task. In setting up systems you should keep in mind:

- Verbal interruptions take up valuable time
- Not all tasks are of equal importance
- Written reports and reporting systems allow you to review performance and evaluate at your own convenience
- Specific methods for reporting help employees gather and have all needed data and cuts time lost in rambling meetings
- Letting the employee know that you are aware the task has been completed is essential
- Organization and attention to detail is a must.

Tools

In back-to-basics management and leadership of all kinds it is important that your mind be as free as possible from any kind of detail that is readily available, e.g. keeping phone numbers at the forefront of your mind uses up valuable thinking space. Here are a few tools that can help:

- Tickler files: Allow you to keep track of the dates that assignments are due.
- Desk and calendar planners: Allow long-range planning and easy to follow agendas at a glance.

- Daily, weekly and monthly agendas: Keep your mind moving and allow you to keep track of your work flow.
- Employee agendas: Allow you to keep track of their work flow and you can check at a glance to see if assignments are being completed.
- Weekly staff or employee meetings (with an agenda): Help you to discover any operating problems and to check up on assigned tasks.
- A system of reporting: This will allow both the employee and yourself to follow the work flow. Include a check off list for easy reading and filling out.

Any one of these may suffice for your needs and you may find that a combination will be very useful.

Without delegation you as a manager will be frantic and your effectiveness will be greatly diluted. Your outlook will be subjective. The other skills required of you will go unused. Delegation is necessary to ensure the continuity of any company. It is through delegation that employees grow, become familiar with policy and learn how to handle authority and leadership. Delegation increases your effectiveness as a back-to-basics manager and leader.

CHAPTER EIGHT

Leadership

> "A manager remains a leader only as long as he keeps proving that he is the superior man with the best method."
> Dr. Kenneth "Thane" Walker

American business in the 80's is suffering from a number of ills. We can point our fingers in many directions. We can look at the lack of proper material investment, lack of foresight in the development of the third world, the arrogant "know-it-all" attitude and the outdated marketing information that has crippled our automobile industry; the inability of top management to use the latest technology in a profitable manner; and the "head in the sand" reactions of union leadership to new productivity methods. All of these, upon close examination, can be traced back to a basic and widely pervasive problem: the lost craft of leadership. It may be a harsh judgment, but all the facts say that many of those in decision-making positions no longer know how to lead their people toward workable, profit-oriented goals.

There are no easy answers to the economic mess we have created. And there are no panaceas and no overnight solutions to our crisis in leadership, either at the national or local level. In doing research on leadership for this book, the authors found an interesting pattern. Published works on leadership appeared around those dates in history when our national situation seemed at a point of crisis and change. During the great Depression, World War II, and the technological revolution of the early 60's, we seemed, as a nation, to be looking for leadership. Now we seem to have lost it again.

Today's crisis in business should be seen in light of fast-moving changes that have pushed young, technologically oriented minds to the forefront of management without any leadership training. A person can be given a position or a title. BUT no one can be given leadership. In order for you to be a back-to-basics manager, you must demonstrate leadership. And to demonstrate leadership, you must give your staff what they want, both consciously and unconsciously.

In *The Leader,* Michael Maccoby reported that *Time* magazine (August 6, 1979) asked a group of prominent Americans to answer the question, "What living American leaders have been most effective in changing things for the better?" Leaders who have given voice to criticisms of traditional leadership such as Ralph Nader and Gloria Steinem were mentioned, but no one named Gerald Ford, Richard Nixon, or Jimmy Carter, or any political leaders. Nor did they agree on leaders of large organizations in business or academia. One person said: "I can't think of any leaders. Isn't this sad? God, that's what's wrong with this country!" That's *exactly* what's wrong.

This little paragraph probably sums up why this chapter is so important to the back-to-basics manager. If most of us don't see those in positions of power as being leaders (and the kind of people they want to emulate), it becomes even more important for those on the rise to understand leadership, and to learn to exercise their power wisely and humanely. Leadership studies are humanistic and philosophical in nature, not scientific. No one has been able to determine in scientific terms whether a leader is born or made. But it is fairly clear that life experiences do have an effect on the quality of leadership. It is also evident that leadership cannot be thrust on someone who is unwilling to take the responsibility. No matter how good leadership is at the top levels of an organization, without wise leadership at all other levels, this top leadership will operate in a vacuum. As a back-to-basics manager, you may have the most direct influence on your corporation. Although everyone looks to top management for policy and corporate direction, it is the day-to-day manager who gives stability to the corporation.

There are many theories as to why more managers do not actively seek leadership positions. Lack of training, lack of role models, the "laid-back" mentality of the 60's and 70's, all play a prominent role. We seem, as Americans, to revere achievement, but back off from the concept of power. As a nation, we do not value power as a socially acceptable attribute. We look warily at those who seek power, and cautiously play down our own power desires. Our suspicions of those in power keep many capable people from seeking those positions, both public and private, where leadership and power come together. It's almost as if we want to have the power without knowing about it, talking about it—and sometimes without *doing* anything about it!

Power in the Management Equation

Like all absolute statements, the time-honored cliche, "power corrupts, absolute power corrupts absolutely," has another side. Powerlessness, according to some psychologists and psychiatrists, is even more corrupting, considering the relative numbers of powerless individuals compared to the powerful. The broadest avenue to power, for most people in society, is stepping up to a management position. There is power at every level of management, but power increases at the higher levels. Effective back-to-basics management demands understanding of the interrelationship of powerful authority figures and those who are subject to this authority, the nominally powerless. We say "nominally," for there are methods by which individuals without nominal authority can exercise either positive influence, e.g., through membership in labor unions or destructive influence through laziness, indifference, absenteeism, antagonism, and even sabotage.

Power is generally recognized as an excellent short-term anti-depressant. There are so many trappings of authority and power that the feeling of enjoyment can range far beyond the department or corporation. Since greater income usually goes with authority, the life style of the family of a powerful man—the schools and colleges, the country clubs, the deference of headwaiters—are among the glamourous trappings of power. In the long term, power and leadership must be seen as a service, responsibility, and an avenue for the betterment of the human condition.

The phrase "a successful leader" needs to be carefully reexamined. We loosely use the word "successful" to describe many activities. We have had successful criminals and successful anti-social leaders, such as Adolf Hitler. These examples may create a bad impression when we think about what a successful leader produces. It seems to say that power always corrupts. But that's *not* the message.

To be successful, today's leaders must show people how to achieve what they want and bring better human good for all. Back-to-basics management must exemplify this type of leadership. We cannot train people in morality or ethics, as these are areas that must be internalized much earlier in our life experiences. Nor are we warning the back-to-basics manager about power. What we are saying is that every manager must come to terms with his personal concept of power. He must see power as a positive aspect of leadership, as a personal responsibility and as a way of leaving the world a better place than the one he was born into.

In one sense, leadership is a matter of degree. A person is a leader to the degree that he:

- Has a following
- The following is voluntary
- Demonstrates that he knows the best method of getting his people what they want
- Is competent at using this method.

The emphasis is on the future. People see leaders as role models. They look at a leader as one who can help them obtain the deep human satisfaction they crave from their work. They will continue to give their loyalty only as long as the leader keeps proving that he is able to supply these satisfactions.

For example, if a business meeting turns out to be non-structured, frustrating, time consumming and achieves no goals, the members will psychologically shift their allegiance from the chairman to the person who seems to offer a more workable way of achieving the objective. Being a leader means that you have the power to shape and mold the present and future of an organization through cooperation of the group. A true leader does not deal with luck but with intelligent organization, delegation, charisma, and a basic understanding of the nature of humankind: the needs, wants, and longings of people on both a conscious and unconscious level. True leaders have some recognizable characteristics and abilities which make them stand out from the crowd. Some are innate; some can be learned.

Here is a leadership "profile."

1. The ability to recognize weakenesses and strengths in one-self and others.
2. The ability to set goals and meet them.
3. The ability to pass on credit to others for their personal contributions.

4. The ability to accept personal responsibility.
5. The ability to find and use the right resource to accomplish a task.
6. The ability to measure the degree of success and failure.
7. The ability to turn every situation into a learning experience.
8. The ability to understand the use of power.
9. The ability to accept a position of power without undue reluctance or zeal.
10. The ability to have a driving force towards personal accomplishment without being self-centered or greedy.
11. The ability to deal with the present in a realistic manner, while dreaming and planning future accomplishments.
12. The ability to maintain a balance between the physical, spiritual and emotional sides of one's life.
13. The ability to plan projects and goals so that they produce a better life for all concerned.
14. The ability to understand that the way a situation is handled is even more important than factual information in achieving good results.
15. The constant drive to know and understand more about everything.
16. The ability to discriminate between truth, wishful thinking and the hard facts.
17. The ability to understand that one's goals and desires are often more complex than those one is leading.
18. The ability to awaken those around them to an understanding of their true potential.

We have fallen into some disastrous misconceptions about what leadership really is. We hear them every day. Such ideas as:

- He is a "born" leader
- Charisma makes a leader
- Conceptual thinking makes for leadership
- Intellect makes a good leader
- Experience makes a good leader
- Innovative ideas make a good leader.

Although any one of the above ideas may work in some situations, they do not, in themselves, make for leadership. In fact, leadership can change with the requirements of a particular situation, i.e., a good sales manager in a highly promotion-type industry may not have acquired the skills needed to lead and manage in an office management situation. The "Peter Principle" often applies to management situations, i.e., an individual who is perfectly competent at one level may not be competent when promoted. The back-to-basics manager-leader should be competent at any level and in any situation because he or she has a basic knowledge of universal leadership and management skills.

Leadership Trends

As conditions and people change, so do styles of leadership. People now seek out new kinds of leaders to help them achieve their goals. Historically, there have been five ages of leadership (and we are presently in a transition period towards the sixth). They include:

1. *Age of Conquest Leadership.* During this period the main threat was conquest. People looked for the leader who was all-powerful; the dominating, masterful ruler who promised people safety in return for their loyalty and taxes.

2. *Age of Commerce Leadership.* By the beginning of the industrial age, safety no longer was the main function of leadership. People began looking for those who could show them how to raise their standard of living. Leaders earned reputations through their skill at bargaining. They usually accumulated vast personal fortunes. This kind of leadership ended as the rulers began to exploit their followers, giving them less and less in return for their performance.

3. *Age of Organization Leadership.* Standards of living rose and were more easily attainable. People started looking for a place to "belong." The measure of leadership became the capacity to organize.

4. *Age of Innovation Leadership.* As the rate of innovation increased products and methods often became obsolete before they were off the planning board. The Age of Organization had created a vehicle that was out of control. The leaders of the hour were those who were extremely innovative and could handle the problems of the increasing speed of obsolescence. These leaders were extremely innovative and creative and kept themselves busy acquiring new knowledge and skills.

New knowledge and skills were used to create new production ideas, marketing concepts and financial means. The industries that had the highest quality of innovative leadership attracted the best creative people. Creative minds did not take jobs because of money but rather to have the chance to work with those who excelled as "thinkers." Fields such as electronics pushed far ahead of other industries and created the need for a new kind of leadership.

5. *Age of Information Leadership.* The last three ages have developed extremely rapidly (starting in the 1920's), and have a great tendency to overlap, depending upon the industry and the company. According to the prestigious research firm of Yankelovich, Skelly and White, Inc., the most powerful force impacting upon us today is our emergence into a knowledge or information society. Increasingly, the result of our work is an information product itself, e.g. the television industry. According to Yankelovich, "organizational and managerial systems that were effective in an industrial setting are no longer appropriate." As technology moves ahead, there is increasing anxiety that we will all be left behind in its electronic wake. It has become clear that no company can survive without leaders who understand and know how to handle information. The modern information leader is the person who is the best information processor; the one who makes the most intelligent sense of information, and uses it in the newest and most creative ways.

6. *Leadership in the "New Age."* The leadership characteristics we described early in this chapter have remained fairly constant throughout this past century. But, we cannot in all honesty accurately predict what special abilities our leaders will need in the future. We can only make educated guesses. Leaders will need to know how to use the new technologies, even though they won't particularly need to know what makes a computer—or other technological improvement—work. They will certainly need to know *how* to think so they can effectively analyze and synthesize the information they will be receiving. Despite new technology, their commitment will remain focused on the individual. They will know that leaders lead people, not things or numbers or projects. They will have

to be able to deliver what people want in order to motivate those they are leading. They will have to develop their listening ability to find out what people want. And they will have to develop their ability to plan, both short term and long term, to keep an edge on the competition. To sum it up, it seems apparent that leaders must do everything they've done before—and then add some new techniques as the "New Age" becomes more firmly established.

You start with a following, and your first test of leadership is making this a *voluntary* relationship (you need their loyalty). Get to know the tangible and intangible needs of everyone in your group. Give them the things that satisfy these needs. This will demonstrate that you know how to get them what they want. Each time you reinforce this idea, they will become a more loyal, a more integrated, more motivated, more cohesive group.

The specific skills you will need are the ability to:

- Process information (not just job information) and use it
- Form premises that lead to useful conclusions
- Be innovative; not creative in the normal sense, but able to do something with the information and resources at hand to give your people a strong competitive edge
- Be able to offer people the options they want in meeting their very special (and very varied) personal needs and desires
- Continue gathering the knowledge and skills that complement your position as a leader.

Rensis Likert's investigations into leadership and management led him to the conclusion that managers must be people-oriented. He found that highly productive managers were more apt to think of people, and in more varied ways. For example, some of the leadership attributes of these high producers were as follows:

- They were good delegators
- They allowed their people to participate in decisions
- They were relatively non-punitive
- They encouraged a two-way communication flow

- They had fewer formal meetings. (They didn't have the need to meet often since the communication flow was good.)
- They were proud of their people, were good motivators, and maintained high morale
- They planned ahead and met their goals
- In times of crisis, they sustained their leadership roles.

One Last Word on Leadership

We are now in the dual age of information and of human rights. As a back-to-basics manager-leader, you must be able to process information and delegate tasks, and at the same time encourage those under you as individuals, regardless of sex, race, and religion. People are a prime natural resource we can no longer afford to waste. Each individual counts—and each one can, if properly motivated, make a specific contribution. Perhaps that is the essential leadership message all managers must learn today.

CHAPTER NINE

Body Language

"The eyes of men converse as much as their
tongues, with the advantage that the ocular
dialect needs no dictionary, but is understood
the world over."
Ralph Waldo Emerson

It is the *recipient* who communicates in the communication process.
The so-called communicator, the person who emits the words does not
communicate. He utters. Unless there is someone to hear there is no
communication; there is only noise. *You* cannot communicate. You
can only make it possible for a recipient to perceive . . . either verbally
or non-verbally.

With the advent of the use of television in political campaigns the
world became aware of the importance of body language and the silent
languages. Today's back-to-basics manager-leader cannot afford to be
unaware of his or her body language and the effect it has on all those
who come in contact with it. In any corporation where the CEO has
frequent contact with lower levels of management, you will notice the
same gestures being used throughout the corporation. These gestures
are more than an unconscious mimicking, they are a way of
communicating corporate policy. The saying "One picture is worth a
thousand words" surely applies to the use and understanding of body
language. The back-to-basics manager-leader must know that his body
language is saying the same thing as his verbal language. He must also
be aware of the conflict in a verbal agreement with an employee when

the employee's body language is making a statement of non-agreement. The back-to-basics manager-leader is always aware that perception (the communication) is not logic but an experience. We always perceive in multiples, never in singular or specifics. These multiples are a part of a whole picture—what we say and what we do at the same time. This "silent language" deals with gestures, tone of voice and the entire environment. The manager-leader must take into consideration the cultural and social implications of those he or she is communicating with. Without this silent language the spoken language cannot communicate successfully.

Many managers have mastered the mysterious task of relating behavior to words by learning to read body language. Just as there is syntax and grammar in the use of language, so there is form and function in each movement a person makes. Knowing about these can be invaluable to the back-to-basics manager-leader. If an employee is truly committed and motivated, the words should not only ring as sincere but the body language should reinforce the spoken language.

Many corporations now spend a great deal of money videotaping their CEOs and others who deal with the public. One reason why this has been so successful is that it enables them to review their body language and improve their overall appearance.

As a back-to-basics manager a great deal of your time is going to be spent talking or listening to and observing others. You, of course, must be able to speak and understand the language of those with whom you are communicating. But if you were to use only spoken language, you would find yourself making many decisions on the basis of information that was incomplete at best. The silent language that accompanies all conversations (and at times carries on a conversation of its own without the spoken word) is extremely important if you are to make valid business decisions. Most people have some awareness of body gestures and react accordingly when speaking and listening to others. But this form of language is so rarely taught to us in formal learning situations that most of what we have learned we know subconsciously. Unfortunately, we often react to this silent information at an unconscious level without true understanding and evaluation. It is important that a back-to-basics manager-leader be as consciously aware as possible of every aspect of his job. The more aware he is the more intelligently he will be able to act. That's what research has shown time and time again.

Management and Body Language

As a manager, a great deal of your time is spent in communicating (approximately 70% of your day). It is no longer enough for you to read body language and interpret symbols at an unconscious level. It becomes important to you to assign meanings to all of these at a conscious level. To the extent you are able to do this, to that extent will you be able to deal effectively with the people who work for and with you.

The Silent Languages

The back-to-basics manager-leader has a basic understanding of the following:

1. *Body gestures.* These include hand movements, coordination, postures, poses, facial expressions (smiles, frowns, searching looks).
2. *Eye motions.* These include movement of the pupils, eye rotation, eyelid opening and closing, blinking. For example, pupils get small and eyes dry in times of fear, anger and hurt. Rapid blinking occurs under stress; open pupils and "dewy looks" occur in times of receptivity, safety and love.
3. *Skin/touch sensations.* This includes how the skin feels to the touch, e.g., cold clammy hands can signal stress (or poor circulation). A limp handshake means lack of enthusiasm and confidence. When people are physically touched, if they tense their muscles it can mean signs of fear and restraint. Ducking motions can mean they perceive (or mistakenly perceive) anger.
4. *Space.* This includes spatial relationships. How a person deals with them is also a non-verbal signal, e.g., do they stand close and lean into others? This can signal interest and comfort with the situation. Stepping back can indicate fear and a feeling of being pressured. Do they build up forts of paper and other items around them as protection?
5. Other aspects of the silent languages include: *environment* (choice of pictures, office appointments and arrangements); *colors* (choices in clothing and schemes in the office); *per-*

fumes and scents (the cosmetic industry has made a vast fortune by understanding the relationship between certain scents and certain personalities).

The idea behind the silent languages is that *all* of these must be combined for proper signals to be read. Most of these signals we read at an unconscious level, and then react.

A warning: Some signals dealing with space, colors and body gestures vary according to what part of the world a person was brought up in. Even in America there can be great differences in how we act depending on our inherited background and the part of the country we came from.

In interpreting body language, you are looking for the overall configuration of signals being sent. The best place to start is by becoming aware of your own silent language in work situations, and noting the connection with your internal feelings. We have included a series of gestures that will help you get started in your exploration.

Body Language

If a manager listens to what a person says and does not look at what that person *does* while saying it, he or she misses the essential mind/body connection. There's a hidden language—body language—that can reveal people's real feelings even when they're not telling the truth. Some study of this language will enable you to read your own gestures and those of your employees like a book. The volatile, imaginative person will generally have a richer store of body language than will the staid, logical person. But everyone will use body language regardless of how many gestures they have in their repertoire. How you choose what part of the body to use and in what way is a personal matter—you'll use the gesture you need at the time.

Warning: Many gestures have more than one meaning, so for an accurate reading it's important to look at body language in context: where it's done, who's present at the time, what preceded it, what followed it. Also remember that body language reflects feelings; as a person's mood changes, so will his body language (i.e. an employee may give one set of signals to you and change dramatically when a peer joins the conversation). Any gesture that's too prevalent in a person's repertoire probably is contrived, deliberately planned for effect. An exaggerated gesture almost always stems from an opposite feeling. The need here is dramatize, so you mask or hide something.

A Glossary of Basic Body Language

Crossing gestures: Any kind of crossing—of legs or arms is a confining gesture, a way of closing the circuits.

Posing: Any artificial, thought-out gesture means, "Look at me and what I have; this is what I am."

Slow, deliberate gestures: This person is monitoring himself, calming his or her mind before zeroing in on one thing at a time. He or she is a planner.

Leaning against something: This person needs contact with his or her surroundings and takes comfort from being near others.

Spreading objects around body: A person who places shopping bags or briefcases around him or her is reaching out and trying to gain more territory.

Lack of movement: A person who's holding his body still is holding it in, hoping no one will notice him or else listening and quietly planning. He's either playing it safe or he is after your job. This person merits watching.

Illustrating with objects vs. illustrating with the body: If a person uses objects on his desk to make a point, he's an outgoing type with his eyes on the ball. He knows what he wants even though he may try not to get too involved. Such people are realists, not dreamers. If they use their fingers or hands to illustrate, they're close to their ideas—nurturing, babying and touching them. They have a very personal approach to things.

Open vs. closed gestures: Generally, open gestures are trusting, while closed ones indicate cutting off or holding back.

Turning towards vs. turning away: Even if only a part of the body—the shoulders, for instance—are turned toward you, it means you're being included in the conversation or situation. A turning away, on the other hand, indicates exclusion.

Leaning forward vs. sitting back: Leaning forward may be a friendly or interested gesture ("tell me more"). Sitting back may indicate a withdrawal of interest ("Let me think about what you just said").

Cocking of the head: Cocking of the head is a sign of interest, of being open and receptive to others' opinions.

Avoidance of eye contact: People who always react this way are unsure of themselves and afraid of you.

Hands folded in lap or on stomach: A protective gesture.

Hands placed on desk: All business—"Let's get right down to it."

Hands on hips: Provocative or tough, flirty or anxious to get down to business. This gesture can also indicate antagonism or a defiant gesture.

Hands in pockets: A feeling of being in touch with one's body, centering oneself. Having the hands contained in a small enclosure is comforting.

Pointing a finger: The person is setting himself or herself up as an authority or is illustrating a point.

Wagging a finger: This is a threat; he or she is antagonizing you, scolding you.

Using the thumb: A power ploy, since the thumb is the seat of power.

Counting on fingers: A logical no-nonsense person, separating the steps in his or her mind as they are presented.

Counting from the thumb: This indicates a forceful presentation.

Counting from the pinkie: This is a softer way of getting ideas across.

Holding fingers straight while pointing, counting: This person has plans framed in his or her mind and knows where to go with them.

Arms folded in front of body: A variety of meanings, depending on the situation. This can be a way of hiding, of holding oneself back, or showing fear and timidity or power and strength (a fortress). Warning: A person with crossed arms may very well just be cold!

Unconvinced

Authoritative

Is it the truth?

Interested, flexible

What was that? Interest has been sparked

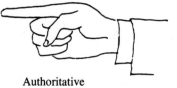

Tough customer

Unsure, frightened, defensive

Authoritative

Threatening, scolding

Stalling for time

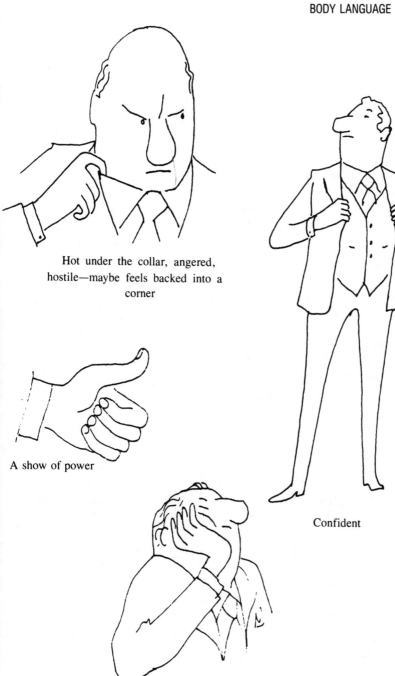

Hot under the collar, angered, hostile—maybe feels backed into a corner

A show of power

Confident

Bored

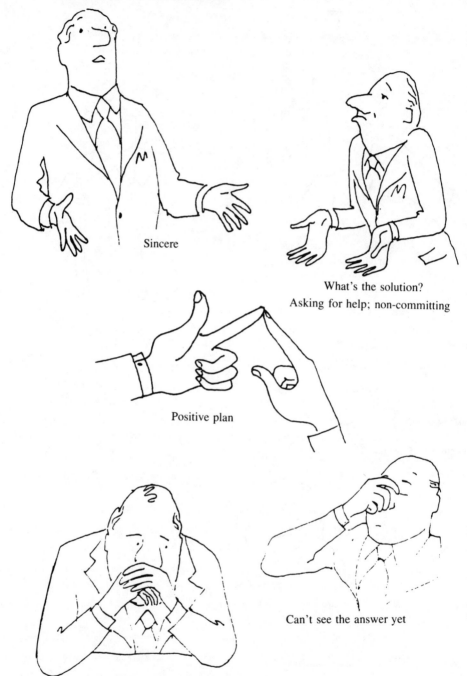

Sincere

What's the solution?
Asking for help; non-committing

Positive plan

Can't see the answer yet

Indecisive; cannot make up his mind

Defensive wall

Obstinate, unsold

Building an idea piece by piece

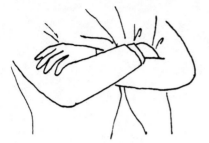

Withdrawing, holding back, fear of power

Feeling of superiority

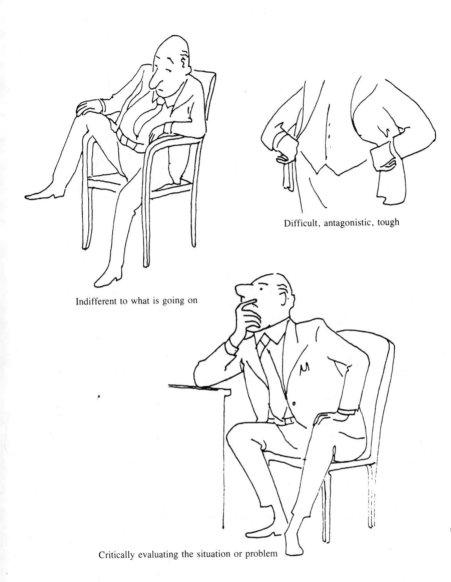

Difficult, antagonistic, tough

Indifferent to what is going on

Critically evaluating the situation or problem

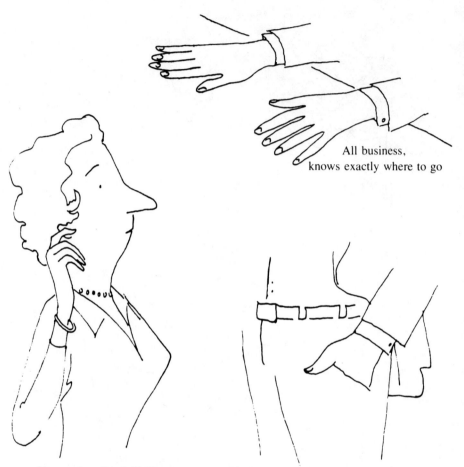

All business,
knows exactly where to go

Interruption (I would like to say something)

closely holding in ideas
Establishing security; being in touch with self

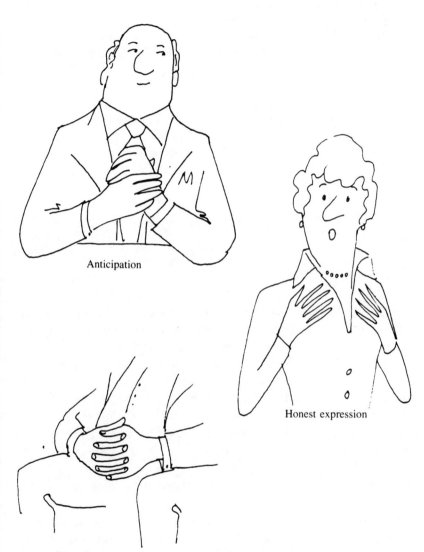

Anticipation

Honest expression

Protectiveness

CHAPTER TEN

Managerial Coaching and Training

"A teacher can only lead you to the threshold of
your own mind."
Kahlil Gibran

Helping people overcome blocks and increase sales, helping clerical staff with new procedures, putting into action new company policies and programs—all of these take a knowledge of education and coaching concepts. It's an extension of training but more personalized, more related to the specific job and the specific individual. But for back-to-basics managers, it's an important and never-ending process.

To coach effectively we must first learn how the mind works. We gather knowledge in two fundamental ways: by rote memories (i.e., the way you learned your multiplication tables in school), or by experience/association (i.e., understanding the meaning of a new word by using it in a sentence). Experience/association learning has been found to be the most effective and long lasting. This means that if someone is to retain knowledge and use it, he must participate actively in the learning process. It has also been found that unless a person can verbalize and articulate the knowledge he is gathering, and relate it in a pragmatic sense, he will not be able to retain or use the information effectively.

In gaining information and relating it to what is already stored, the mind works in a very logical manner. It gathers information in sentences or statements of facts (called the *major premise*). The next step is an associative statement (called the *minor premise*). From this point it draws a *working conclusion* (upon which action is based). It is important to note that if the major premise is erroneous, the conclusion will also be erroneous; i.e., all lawyers are crooks, (major premise) John Doe is a lawyer, (minor premise); therefore John Doe is a crook (working conclusion). Our actions are then based on the idea the John Doe is a crook. Our major premise was erroneous because we formulated a *general statement* that was contrary to fact. Once the major premise has been set and minor premise given, the mind inevitably reaches the conclusion.

What to Do

As a back-to-basics manager, it will be a very rare occasion when you have to set up a formal training or coaching situation. But on a daily basis you will find many times when you will find yourself educating your people. The process is relatively simple, and will become part of your thinking and behavior as you begin to use it. The process is as follows:

- *A statement of facts and information.* Keep it short and introduce one idea at a time. Pick out the prime idea that the concept is based on.
- *A statement of association.* State how this information is to be used, or if it is to be used in conjunction with current procedures. Ask those you are speaking with to add to this statement.
- *Ask those you are training to draw conclusions and express them aloud.* Spend some time letting them articulate until they show they have grasped the information and understand how it is to be used. Example: *Major premise:* We are adding a new area to our company's information services department. *Minor premise:* The procedure will be the same as you are now using. Unspoken conclusion: this will be easy for me to understand since I already know those procedures. At this point the employee is open, receptive and following you. You are now ready to introduce information and get feedback. You have done two things. First of all you have started the trainee thinking in a logical manner. Second, you have started to introduce the information in an

experience/association manner. The trainee will continue to think in this manner.

Learning Blocks

Learning blocks can occur in a variety of areas. The most important indication is the inability to articulate the information in a manner that is useful and pragmatic. This can be caused by fear, lack of communication skills, information not being presented in a logical manner, or lack of association/experience with the material being presented. If the trainees have no previous experience with procedures or information, their learning period will have to include a trial-and-error step before they become accustomed to what is being introduced. Emotional blocks (learning to do something one way and not being able to see other ways) will also take some considerable relearning.

Communication and Learning

We act according to the non-verbal pictures we draw in our minds, which we then translate into words and actions. In training and coaching, the best method for getting ideas across is the use of words that will help us draw pictures (80% of our learning is visual). Rather than speaking is absolutes and abstractions, speak in those common words that will draw pictures in the mind (e.g., instead of saying, "learning is an understanding process," use "learning is like bringing a picture into focus on a slide projecor; it lets you see the picture and what is really going on"). Use universal analogies and metaphors. In communication and training it is important to be able to find common points of understanding and relatedness. Universal concepts deal with nature, human experience and cultural fields such as music and art. Try not to speak in terms of good and bad. This immediately sets up judgment blocks and conclusion blocks and leads to tension and fear of making mistakes.

Keep the atmosphere relaxed and open. Keep away from the traditional classroom approach. If training in groups, try to keep seating arrangement in circles or horse-shoe shapes. If dealing on a one-to-one basis, come out from behind your desk. Use visual aids such as slides or flip charts to make points. Video tapes and television can also be used but since they have soporific effects they should not be used for longer than 15 minutes at a time.

If you must lecture, remember that the normal attention span is very limited; 50% of your audience's attention may wander in the first five minutes of your talk. Unless you are extremely entertaining and graphic in your words, you should go no longer than 20 minutes. Speak slowly and clearly. Use voice modulations—monotones are deadly and will put everyone to sleep within minutes. Use body language gestures. Make eye contact often. Use first names instead of "you" if possible.

Encourage trial and error in conversation. Don't criticize "stupid answers" and "wrong conclusions." They may indicate a natural process of assimilating information in the mind.

What are your counseling/coaching objectives?

1. To make your staff aware of their strengths so their effective behavior is reinforced
2. To help them understand what improvement they need, and how they can bring it about (with your help)
3. To help them see the relationship between their own needs and the needs of the company
4. To demonstrate that their needs and the company's needs can both be satisfied by improved performance
5. To help them set priorities and develop action plans for achieving their improvement goals.

To illustrate, let's go through the various phases of a counseling/coaching session. It goes something like this.

Initial Action: Staff member is told what the interview is about, and what he can expect to get out of it. It is made clear that the session will be a joint venture in which he is expected to participate. The back-to-basics manager approaches this as objectively as he can. He is candid, open-minded, and eager to help. He conveys respect for the staff member—with the goal always businesslike and result-oriented.

Communicating: The prerequisite of all effective communication is that is be two-way and interactional. The employee is encouraged to talk by your obvious willingness to listen. Be sure your communication is balanced, focusing on pluses as well as minuses. Your objective is for the employee to finish the interview with greater self-awareness than he had at the start. Basically the effective back-to-basics manager communicates successfully because he shows that he *wants* to know what the employee says—and he respects what is being said.

Direction of Interview: The manager should guide the counseling/ coaching interview towards a specific goal. This requires great skill, because he must bring the employee to the goal without coercion or manipulation. It must be a shared conclusion. Remember, coaching is not a negative. It is a highly effective way of changing a productive employee into a still more productive one, and an excellent one into a superstar.

Conclusion

With the swift movement forward of our technological society, our universities geared up to handle the education process required for this movement. In doing so the emphasis on such topics as leadership (which would normally be found in a liberal arts education) was pushed into the background. It takes only common sense to realize that without this type of education America cannot remain a world leader in any area. Consequently it falls on the shoulders of the back-to-basics-manager-leader to train those under them in basic leadership skills. Leadership skills are learned for the most part through informal education processes and in many cases through emulation until the student of leadership has formed an internal knowledge and understanding of the skill. The back-to-basics manager-leader must be constantly aware of the work place as a training ground for those who will eventually replace him.

CHAPTER ELEVEN

Communication Skills

"If people around you will not hear you, fall
down before them and beg their forgiveness, for
in truth you are to blame."
Feodor Dostoyevski

The ability to communicate skillfully and effectively is a central part of
everything a manager does. Most "people" problems can be traced in
part or in full to poor communication, a breakdown in communication,
a misunderstanding about what communication is or no
communication at all. Human interaction succeeds or fails as a direct
result of our ability to communicate.

Let's start by defining communication. It is not easy because
communication is not a thing—it's a process. And it is the very process
that is its essence. What is this process? It is composed of five links,
each of which must be present in order for effective communication to
occur. They are: "Who—Says what?—To whom?—Through what
medium? With what effect?" Let's define them.

1. *Who?* This is the communicator. His or her status, reputation,
previous ability to communicate are all factors in weighing the listener
or reader's desire to hear or read what he or she has to say this time.

2. *Says what?* This refers to the content of the message itself. To be
effective, a communication must appeal to the audience's needs and
expectations. Information by itself has no meaning. People give it
meaning only by what they perceive.

3. *To whom?* This is your audience. We have already spoken about the importance of understanding needs and drives. This is especially true if you want to get your message across. Communication is perception—it's only what the other fellow hears, sees and is moved by that counts. In effect, there is no communication until and unless the recipient is involved.

4. *Through which medium?* The late Marshall McLuhan made this point famous when he said, "The medium is the message." You know that from your own experience. A message delivered on television is not the same as the identical message delivered on radio or in print. And in your own functioning as a manager, the uniqueness of verbal persuasion as a channel of communication must be understood and acted upon.

5. *With what effect?* This is the payoff. True communication demands that the recipient become somebody, do something, believe something. It always strives for motivation. Something has to happen or communication has not taken place. Communication is two-way—and you've got to have some kind of feedback to know if you have succeeded.

In a sense, the person who receives the message is the "communicator"—because unless he or she does something about it, communication has not been achieved. It is the same as the old story about a tree falling down in the wilderness. Is there a sound if there's nobody around to hear it? The sound waves create action but there's no reaction. Communication demands both. It's a humbling thought when you think of all the fine writing, talking, pictures we produce—but it's the truth. Think about it in this context and you'll be way ahead of most managers.

There are generally four stages of growth that an individual goes through in developing his or her communication skills. They are:

1. You feel guilty about the roadblock you may have been putting up in the ways others communicate. Don't let this guilt get in your way. Did you feel guilty because you didn't know how to ride a bike? Keep trying!

2. You feel phony. Everyone feels phony when they start practicing a new skill. Remember your first sales call or first speech? You felt "wooden" and "artificial!" But the feeling soon goes away.

3. With practice, most people learn listening skills rather rapidly. You will be aware at a conscious level of what you are doing for some time before it becomes a part of you.
4. The skills will finally become integrated into your psychological makeup. At that point, you will be able to do them well, with little conscious awareness that you are using them.

Honest, open communication can be one of the most rewarding experiences in anyone's life. Always remember—good communication is good business and the first step in effective leadership.

The Importance of Effective Communication

As we can see, getting a message from one head into another is not easy. Possibilities of communication breakdown occur all along the process just described. Cutting down or eliminating these breakdowns is your responsibility as a manager. We all know that ROI is an acronym standing for return on investment, which is a vital concern for any business person. But ROI can also mean return on *individuals*. Managers manage people—and the art of management is concerned with realizing the maximum return from each individual. Communication is the primary tool with which this is accomplished. And in order to be effective, you've got to understand that communication is more than talking. It is, in fact, inseparable from your total behavior. The effectiveness with which a manager communicates depends upon his verbal skills, his listening skills, his observational skills, his attitudes towards his people, the non-verbal signals he gives off and his ability to persuade people to take action.

What Can a Manager Do?

As we have just illustrated, communication is a complicated affair—and a very personal one. See if these ideas help you establish more meaningful relationships with your people.

• How you view the relationship between yourself and other individuals determines (to a great extent) how you will function within it. Creating the climate in which a relationship can function is primarily the manager's responsibility. A meaningful relationship *must* be initiated by you, the manager.

- If you are to establish an effective relationship, you should avoid the tendency to communicate because of your title, position or status. You've got to share objectives, values, attitudes and interests. Without a sense of community and sharing, attempts to establish interaction are fruitless.
- When trying to understand the self-concept of another person, try to adopt the person's frame of reference, and be mindful of his viewpoint even if it differs from yours. This means more than that old cliche about putting yourself in someone else's shoes; it is more like getting into his skin, thinking his thoughts, seeing his world, feeling his feelings. Thinking about another person is fine, but thinking and feeling with him is far more productive.

As a manager your goal is to communicate, not to impress. You are not trying to "win" but to develop a team that will achieve mutual goals. You may be able to dictate the manner of communication, but you have no way of commanding a certain response. In effect, the listener controls the speaker. The listener decides if he or she wants to hear, or read, or be motivated. Not *you*. That's something you should always keep in mind—and it is a fact of life that should *always* shape the way you communicate.

Meanings Are in People

The essential point to remember is that words, as symbols, provide the vehicles through which we can transmit ideas and information. But words themselves are not the information that we are transmitting. They are not things, behavior or feelings—they are only a system of symbols. Before we can use words effectively, we must first understand the nature of meaning.

Words do not have intrinsic meanings. They "contain" meanings as a glass contains water. Dictionaries give us the definitions of words, not the meanings. Meanings are highly individual and personal. Many disagreements and arguments occur when people have different definitions for a word, and each is sure his or her meaning is the "right" one.

The points to remember are: (1) meaning is a very private affair, and (2) individuals cannot have identical experience in any given situation.

We must accept the probability that no two people can ever completely grasp a meaning in the same way. Accepting this concept encourages us to seek ways to clarify messages—and prevents us from placing the blame for miscommunication on the other fellow. You should always remember that when you communicate, you are not transmitting meanings, only symbols. Before any communication takes place, you should answer these six questions—and shape your message accordingly:

(The first three apply to you as the sender.)
1. What do I intend to communicate?
2. What will I actually communicate?
3. What do I really mean, and what will be the emotional impact of what I communicate?

(The other three questions apply to the receiver.)
1. What does he expect to hear?
2. What might he hear, despite what is being said?
3. How will he feel about what he hears?

What we are highlighting here is the reciprocality of communication flow. No matter what the message intent or content, no matter how creative or clever we are, the only way we know if a communication is effective is through the feedback we get from it. Feedback is absolutely necessary to complete the communication loop, and to provide for the verification of meaning from the receiver back to the sender. Only by knowing the results of our communication can we alter or correct the message so we can achieve our desired goal, or response, from the receiver.

Sharpening Communication Skills

This next section is a series of "how-to's" concerned with building your individual communication skills. This is particularly important, because recent surveys show that managers spend almost 70% of their time in some form of communication activity. Of this, the highest percentage of time is spent in listening—which is why we devoted a full chapter to that oft-neglected skill. The other key skills of speaking, writing and making the most of meetings will be discussed here.

The Art of Verbal Persuasion

Verbal persuasion is certainly not a one-way street. The old idea of the hard-sell spellbinder has been out for ages (if it ever was in). It helps to think of verbal persuasion as a game. When you're talking, you're not talking in a vacuum, you're always competing with the inner voice of the other person. For example, you may be speaking to one of your salespeople who is still dreaming about the last big sale he made. Is he listening? Not really. Not until you capture *all* of his attention. Not until you make it important to him. Not until you get *him* involved.

But the good news is that reaching minds, and hearts, is a skill that anyone can acquire—if they work at it, if they remember that verbal persuasion is a process, if they make sure that what they say:

- Is heard by their listeners
- Is understood
- Holds his interest
- Gets him involved
- Leads to action!

A tall order? Not really. We do it all the time. But most of us can improve dramatically if we work on our skills. Here are some suggestions based on extensive psychological research:

- Present one idea at a time. One point of information; one idea; one reason why. Simple? No! To be effective, each single point must have a variety of attributes as follows:
  1. *Making the Statement*
     Use simple words.
     Use accurate words.
     Make it interesting.
     Make it brief.
  2. *Develop the Idea*
     Explain it.
     Illustrate it.
     Show it in action.
     Invite questions.
  3. *Restate the Idea*
     Sum it up.
     Check up on understanding.

4. *Call to Action*
    Suggest agreeement.
    Get *action!*

- Say it simply. You'll come across to your listener if the words you use fulfill these requirements:
  1. You know what the words mean.
  2. Your listener knows what the words mean.
  3. Both of you agree on the meaning of the words. The point is that the best way to make things understood is to say them *as simply as possible.*

- Make it brief. Most of us talk too much. Why? Because it's easier to talk around a subject than to hit right on. Here are some ways to economize on your words:
  1. Eliminate add-ons.
  2. Avoid saying the same thing twice.
  3. Cut overtalk.
  4. Dodge verbal detours.
  5. Check wordiness.

- Word pictures help you. Make it easy for your listener to picture what you say. How?
  1. Personalize and localize.
  2. Talk about him and what he knows.
  3. Stay clear of negatives.
  4. Ask, don't tell—so he'll draw *his* picture in his mind.

- Get acceptance of one idea before moving on to the next. Listening without protest does not necessarily imply acceptance. It can simply mean that the idea may not have penetrated, or it could have been twisted by the listener into something he wanted to hear, or that he could accept more readily. Get some positive reaction to one thought or idea before moving on to the next.

The foregoing techniques all deal with transmitting ideas from one person to another. This is not the whole story of communication, however. Motivating the other person to listen, to evaluate with an open mind, to respond with his ideas and feelings and to do what you request are the other crucial factors. For example:

- Be responsive to emotions. In any discussion, a current of feeling flows as ideas are exchanged among the participants. These expressions of feeling are woven into the fabric of the conversation, sometimes so subtly as to be almost indistinguishable from the threads of ideas. However, they must be responded to. How? With the manager's communication tools—encouragement, reassurance and praise.

- Encourage expression. When the other person expresses emotion, try to draw him out. The more he releases the pent-up tension from the emotion, the more comfortable he'll be—and the readier to listen to what you say.
- Sympathize and empathize. An important contribution to rapport is made when you express appreciation of the other person's feeling. When he expresses anger or anxiety, it is wise for you to tell him that you understand the way he feels. This has nothing to do with whether or not he is justified in his feelings or whether or not you would feel the same way. You are merely expressing sympathy. And sympathy sparks communication.
- Give of yourself. When you share your ideas and feelings with another person, he is motivated to respond in a similar manner. This results in getting richer communication from the other person. The idea that the less the other person knows about you the better leads to a strained relationship that goes nowhere fast.

One last point to remember. Skill in verbal persuasion can be developed only through practice. As with all skills, just knowing the rules is not enough. Practice! Practice! Practice!

The Skill of Writing

As managers, speaking and listening dominate a large part of our communication endeavors. However, a skill that is often undervalued is that of writing. Many of us would just as soon shy away from the subject. We consider writing an unpleasant chore. Even answering a simple letter can be a traumatic experience. Although we may want to avoid it, writing is a fact of life for every manager. Most managers spend at least 10% of their communication time in some form of writing. So we might as well do it right. Especially since writing is a craft that requires effort and understanding more than inspiration.

A good way to start thinking about writing is to remember that just because you write something is not a good enough reason for people to read it. If you keep in mind how may pieces of paper flood onto our desks, you'll understand that before people will read, you've got to capture their attention. Any written communication must follow the rules painstakingly developed by the experts in this field. For example:

- Command attention. Something has to make the potential reader stop what he or she is doing and read what you've written.
- Arouse interest. Getting attention is only the first step. You've got to push the reader's "hot button" to get him or her interested.
- Involve the reader. Any good writing is a one-to-one communication. You're not writing to a group, even though a group of people may read it. Think of your audience as one person. It will improve your style.
- Call to action. That's the writer's equivalent of asking for the order. The basic purpose of a business message is to secure favorable response or willing acceptance from the people to whom it has been directed. If it does not accomplish this, then it is worthless, regardless of the time and effort you spent preparing and writing it.

We need to be aware of the fact that written language is quite different from spoken language. Can you imagine yourself saying: "In reply to your recent inquiry, please be advised that an investigation was conducted and the materials in question were discovered." Of course not! You'd say "We found it!" Written language is usually more formal, but we should not let questions of grammatical structure distract us from our objective. We need to adjust our language to what is most meaningful to our readers. The ultimate criterion exists not in the product itself, but rather in the reader's reaction to it. (Yes, we've said that before but it bears repeating.)

Those in the direct-mail business, whose very livelihood depends on their skill with words, have come up with an interesting formula for getting across to people in print. Here's how it goes:

1. Promise a benefit.
2. Enlarge on the benefit.
3. Tell the reader specifically what he will get, should do, etc.
4. Go into detail, backing up your benefit promises with proof.
5. Tell the reader what he might lose if he doesn't act *now*.
6. Rephrase your reader benefit.
7. Incite to action now!

Is that limited to direct mail? No. Try it in memos and you'll create real dynamite!

The Skill of Letter Writing

Writing letters is an important managerial skill. Again, there are certain fundamentals that will help *anyone* improve. The first step is making your meaning clear. Take care of this and, for the most part, the grammar will take care of itself. Remember—effective communication is your goal, not winning the Shakespearian Society's award. Get your ideas in order. Select the right words. Be concise. Be sincere. Use all of the attention-getting devices available on a typewriter: underlining, CAPITALIZATION, indenting, imaginative punctuation. It *works!*

Before you send out your letter, ask yourself these questions:

- Is it reader-oriented? Have you considered the reader's interests?
- Is it tactful? Are you courteous? Have you put yourself in the reader's place?
- Is it clear and concise? Do your sentences generally contain no more than one main idea? Are these ideas linked with strong transitions? Do you avoid technical terms that may not be clear to your reader?
- Is it conversational? Do you avoid commercial and business English, and use words and phrases from your everyday speaking vocabulary?
- Is it helpful? Have you anticipated and met the reader's needs? Have you given him useful information he may not have expected?
- Have you affected your reader agreeably? Have you created good will?

If you can answer yes to each of these questions, send the letter. It will do the job for you!

Making the Most of Meetings

Although many of us moan and groan about meetings, they are a vital part of corporate life. So we might as well accept them. And, when they are *our* meetings, we should try to improve them. Much of the criticism leveled against group discussions stems from a lack of understanding of crucial group forces and the complexities of group leadership. Meetings, if handled properly, give participants an opportunity to interact and develop into an effective team. They provide an opportunity for your people to share their experiences, viewpoints, problems and successes. Properly conducted, meetings can accomplish several communication and managerial purposes at one time. They can keep people informed, solve problems, discover attitudes and provide a participative climate. As a manager, you may find yourself applying more of the principles of communication in meetings than in any other managerial activity.

Why Meetings?

The meeting serves a number of important purposes. It is basically a pooling together of information, knowledge, facts, opinions and judgments of the participants in order to accomplish a specific purpose. Problem-solving is another reason for holding meetings. That old adage that two heads are better than one still seems to hold. Sharing decisions and policies are good reasons for holding meetings. The fact that meetings are necessary and are used extensively does not mean that they are always effective. Many meetings are badly organized and poorly conducted and are therefore almost totally useless. Another kind of useless meeting is one in which the leader uses the meeting to confirm his decision. Having made up his mind, he uses the meeting to rubberstamp his own conclusions.

Some organizations continue to hold meetings out of habit rather than need. There *has* to be a reason for getting people together, or else forget it. Here are some things to think about before calling another meeting:

1. Don't call a meeting if the matter can be resolved some other way.
2. Make the purpose of the meeting known to everyone who is coming.
3. Invite only those who are needed at the meeting.
4. Start at the time announced.
5. Stop when the purpose of the meeting has been achieved.
6. Prepare your agenda in advance.
7. Keep to your agenda.

8. Schedule far enough ahead so everyone has a chance to think about the meeting's objectives.
9. Cancel if the need for the meeting disappears.

What Exactly Is a Meeting?

A meeting is a dynamic group process which is fluid, inexact, changing, and impossible to reduce completely to a set of patterns and descriptions. These qualities should not be regarded as negatives, but rather as the meeting's chief assets. A well-functioning group is never static. Any group of people coming together to pool their knowledge and opinions, needs and hopes, trusts and fears creates an exceedingly dynamic phenomenon; it changes from minute to minute as the interaction unfolds. Every meeting has style and personality all of its own. It is made up of individual human beings, each of whom brings to the meeting his or her own personality, values, feelings and needs. When these individuals combine in a meeting, they become something more than the sum total of the individual members. This "group personality" will influence the way in which the members will participate and relate to each other.

How to Get a Discussion Going

As the manager, you will undoubtedly be the leader in your group. It therefore becomes your responsibility to get people to participate in the discussion. The best technique to achieve this is by asking questions. Here are 8 types of questions you can ask:

1. fact-finding
2. cause and effect
3. leading questions (these suggest answers)
4. provocative (playing the devil's advocate)
5. direct (at a specific person)
6. relayed (bounced to group)
7. reflected (returned to the asker)
8. open-ended (very general, permits discussant to pick his topic).

The magic, all-purpose question to clear the air and keep discussion going is, "Will you give us an example to show what you mean?"

Handling Difficult Situations:

- *When one or two individuals dominate the group:* Ask them for specific information and examples. Direct and relay questions to other members. Set time limits for individual speaking. After the meeting, talk to them individually.
- *When some members will not talk:* Ask them directly for an opinion. Direct some easy questions their way. Be careful not to embarrass them. Get other members of the group to draw them out.
- *When there is an obvious lack of interest:* Drop the topic and move to another point. Ask for, or give, a specific illustration. Use provocative questions (and other types, too). Introduce humor. Take a break.
- *When the discussion drifts off the subject.* Bring discussants back to the point with questions. Give an illustration or case example back on the topic. Summarize and go on to the next topic. Appoint a member of the group as a pilot to keep the group on course.
- *When conflict occurs:* Leaders should *never* take sides! Remind the group of areas of agreement. Remind the group that intelligent people have different opinions. (This makes horse trading possible.) Use humor to relieve tensions. Tell them that the real fun of discussion comes in trying to understand the other fellow's point of view.
- *When the leader makes an obvious mistake:* Admit it, and laugh at yourself. Ask the group for help. Above all, stop doing what you are doing and try something else.

Your Duties as Chairperson

As chairperson, you must recognize that it takes a lot of work and a lot of skill to keep a meeting going constructively. Here are some of the things you are responsible for:

- Keeping the discussion focused on one agenda item at a time.
- Cutting off discussion (or debate) when it becomes redundant
- Ensuring that everyone can be heard from—and controlling the "dominator"
- Keeping the atmosphere relaxed and informal—and using Robert's "Rules of Order" to reach a conclusion

- Being able to know when to delegate to "volunteers"
- Making sure the agenda items are everyone's business—if an item involves only you and one other person it is not committee business
- Encouraging full discussion (that may mean heated debate); hearing the minority viewpoint; serving as negotiator and arbitrator; and staying neutral
- Listening better than anyone else
- Keeping your temper
- Adjourning on time!

CHAPTER TWELVE

Managerial Goal Setting

"A man without a dream and a plan is a man
without a future."
Dr. Kenneth "Thane" Walker

Goals are internalized dreams, and the steps necessary to accomplish
these dreams are called plans and objectives. From early childhood
most people are taught the importance of setting goals and plans. You
are told this is important to your future. But why? In this chapter we
explain not only why they are important to you as a person, but also as
a back-to-basics manager involved with setting goals that work and
producing plans that can be followed by other people.

The Mechanism of the Mind

Research done in the late 50's and early 60's at Duke, Stanford and
Johns Hopkins universities revealed some important information about
how the mind works. The studies showed that the conscious mind is
the intellectual, logical, no-memory side of our life, while the
unconscious mind holds all memory, deals in dreams and pictures, and
dictates all actions to the conscious mind. It also showed that
consciously we can tell the unconscious mind what to do, and it in turn
tells our conscious mind and sets us into *action*.

The unconscious mind is powerful, motivated by past experiences; it colors and causes our behavior. Here are some characteristics of the unconscious mind you should be aware of:

- It does not act on logic but on remembered experiences.
- It does not know the difference between daydreams, mental visual pictures and reality.
- It acts like an autopilot, automatically setting the whole internal system into action.

What does all of this mean to the back-to-basics manager? It means that unless you have a visual picture of what you would like your future to be, unless you have specific plans (written) with the steps figured out, those dreams and plans may not come to fruition. Goals are the internalized drives that make all of us go.

Some people are born with the ability to plan and organize their lives, others are searching for misplaced articles from the very beginning. Some participants in management seminars are able to pick up the ideas presented on planning and proceed immediately with a sense of direction, while others are seemingly unable to comprehend the ideas. It is important to understand that these individuals do not suffer from lack of will or conviction. They just seem to lack organization. it does not appear to be a matter of early training, but more a matter of internal process. Some of the disorganized managers tell us that both parents were organized and tried to instill this into their lives.

Disorganization has often been linked in our thinking to the genius, the creative inventor, the writer and the artist. When we think of these highly creative people we often draw mental pictures of rooms in total confusion, with the artist working at whim when an idea comes to him. This misperception may have become a part of the creative mystique surrounding many who produce new ideas and concepts for the world. But those who have been the most productive will tell you that creative genius is 90% work and 10% talent. They are very organized, have a great sense of self-discipline and are highly goal-oriented.

Some of the common myths about planning are as follows:

- Being organized will keep me from thinking creatively.
- Too many emergency situations occur for me to plan effectively.
- Planning and being organized takes too much time.

- I can't plan in these uncertain times.
- If I plan and organize, I may develop tunnel vision and thereby miss other opportunities.
- I may look confused, but I know where everything is, and what I should be doing, even if no one else does.

IMPORTANT: Being organized means that, as a back-to-basics manager, your business systems and plans are so well planned that others could step in and do the job without missing a beat.

Business cannot afford to maintain people who make themselves "indispensable" because of the lack of formal planning and organization.

Where to Start:

1. Job descriptions are a must. You must have on paper a description of what your job entails as well as that of each person reporting to you. Write a paragraph or make a list of your duties and what you are expected to do. Also list how often these functions are to be done, and how long each function will take to complete. Have the people who work for you do this same exercise and give you the results.
2. Clean house: Do your files; clean off your desk. Try never to leave work with a messy desk or papers left on the desk. Urge your people to do the same.
3. Be sure you have the right equipment. Any office supply store can furnish you with equipment such as phone files, in/out baskets, pencil/pen holders, desk top organizers, etc.
4. Tabulate time. Take your duty list and group chores together in categories, i.e., daily, bi-weekly, weekly, bi-monthly, monthly, quarterly, semi-annually, annually.

Use a monthly planning calendar to write in daily chores. Make a notation of the amount of time each task is estimated to take. Go to your bi-weekly list and decide (by looking back over your appointment calendar) which days these tasks are/should be done and fill in the days with time indicated. Repeat this task until you have covered the entire year for your prescribed duties. If you are not sure of what your daily duties are (even the small incidentals) make a list of what you do for two weeks with the amount of time indicated. Add any personal items that must be handled during working hours to this planning calendar, i.e., physical exercise, banking, etc. Make sure you have put office house-keeping chores (for you or your staff) on the calendar. Office files should be updated at least once every six months, some files put into storage once a year etc.

IMPORTANT: The key to being organized is not the notations you have made on the planning calendar, but the self-discipline you need to use the system. Disorganized managers find themselves up against a deadline or missing business because they let work pile up to the last minute, and do not plan for interruptions. There are emergencies in most organizations, but the key to remaining organized is never to deviate too long from your plan. For instance, you can go two days without doing your daily tasks, but you should not go a third; you can skip a weekly task once, but you should not skip it twice and should never skip monthly, quarterly and annual planning. If the quarterly report takes eight hours, start the project two weeks before it is due. That way you can skip a couple of days if you have an emergency to handle. In the period of time you are working on the quarterly report it becomes a daily chore and is added to your planning calendar in this manner.

Hints:

- It may take you as long as six months (especially if you have been disorganized your whole life) before you become truly organized and feel comfortable with it.
- Always put everything back in its proper place as you finish with it.
- Leave your desk clean and orderly when leaving the office for lunch and for the night.
- Urge that your people leave their desk/work areas clean and orderly.
- Carry out a desk check with employees to see once a month if all work is being put where it belongs. Only those employees who work on sensitive material should have locked desks. Someone must have a master key to get to information if there is an emergency. All employees should be allowed an area of their desk to keep personal items and this area may be locked, but again a master key should be available to you for inspection and

to make sure needed files and information are not in the wrong place. In many companies the head of personnel carries out the desk check on clerical help and holds a master key.

- Research shows that it takes about 21 days to make and break habits. You will need to be very diligent until you have formed new habits within your organization.
- If your household and personal life are disorganized, apply the same principles to help you there. It will make it much easier to follow through on the job.
- Learn to say "no" if you are asked to take on tasks outside of your normal duties. Many times you will not have a choice in a business situation, but good communication and time planning will help you explain the situation to your superior. It is better to have an honest talk than unfinished or delayed projects on your record.
- Insist that your people use the same methods to become organized.
- Talk to a friend, peer or anyone that you can use as a support system. If need be, set up a system of reporting your progress on a daily basis.

If you have organized yourself, you are now ready to start planning. Your planning calendar will become the basis for your daily agenda and a start towards setting long-term plans in motion.

Where to Start?

You start by taking a Saturday afternoon with a journal, yearly, monthly and daily planner and two or three hours of uninterrupted time. Take a look at the "whole" you. Look at your image, goals and motivations. Do your personal and business goals mesh? Form a picture in your mind of what and where you would like to be at retirement age, both financially and personally.

Steps to take are:
- Form a mental picture of your future.
- Write down in your journal your financial goals at retirement and your personal goals.
- Set goals (very specific) in time sequences (lifetime, 10 years, 5 years, 1 year, 6 months, 1 month).

- Make a list of what must be done in order to achieve those goals.
- Write these in your monthly planner on a daily basis, in sequence, so you can start looking at what you must do this month in order to achieve what you have planned; write your plans and goals as if someone else were going to carry them out; the more *detail* you give your plans the better.
- Fill in daily, monthly and yearly dates so you'll know when steps must be taken in order to fulfill your plans.
- Try setting goals in each of these areas: career, physical, family, personal attitude, financial, public service, educational and entertainment.

Goals on a Daily Basis

The key to effective goal setting is to work on your goals every day. Anyone in a management position has what could be termed "emergencies." During an emergency your system gears itself up. Once the emergency is over, the tendency is to feel let down. Great amounts of time are wasted during this period "getting back into the routine." Daily planning and goal setting will help eliminate time wasters. They keep the whole system pointed in the direction of action that is needed to run your business and your life efficiently.

Here are some suggestions:
- Take 5 to 10 minutes at the end of each day to make out a "to do" list for the coming day.
- List the projects under 3 headings: "Must do," "Should do," "Would like to do."
- Any item that can be delegated, or should be delegated, pull off and put on another list with the name of the person to whom you are going to delegate it.
- Leave nothing to memory; add phone calls, lunches, checking on projects, etc.
- On each list qualify projects according to priority.
- Check your list the first thing in the morning *before leaving for the office* (no matter what is happening when you reach the office, you will be aware of what needs to be done).
- Once every hour for 3 to 5 minutes close your door, take no phone calls or interruptions; clear you head and check off your list. Rearrange priorities if necessary; add what is needed.

(Three to 5 minutes of uninterrupted time each hour can increase your efficiency as much as 50%.)

- When forming your "to do" list, add any carry-over projects from the day before. Make sure you also have a space for long-time projects.
- Keep your lists for one month. At the end of the month see what has been accomplished; take a good look at what could be eliminated and what you could be delegating.
- At the end of each month make a plan for the following month. Set down your monthly goals in writing at the top of the plan. On your daily planner mark what day a project must be started in order to be accomplished, and what day it should be finished. As you do your daily "to do" list you can add these from your daily planner.
- Make sure you set aside at least 3 hours during every working week for some form of physical exercise.

Why Some Goals Don't Work

Some common reasons why planning doesn't work are as follows:

- Too many items per day (causing feelings of confusion and being overloaded).
- Not setting priorities, or seeing too many areas as being priorities.
- The non-completion syndrome (not being able to complete even small projects gives feelings of failure). Finish everything that you possibly can. Start with a small area and work up if necessary.
- Inability to visualize self-completing goals or to see a finished situation. Learn to take time to see yourself as a winner. For example, if you play a sport and always lose to a certain competitor, learn to see and feel yourself winning the next match. You cannot accomplish what you cannot visualize.
- Lack of self-esteem, self-confidence, self-motivation, self-discipline.
- Fear of success. Most people recognize the fear of failure. The fear of success can be just as demoralizing. It also comes from deep feelings; fear of "How would I act?" fear of added

responsibility, fear of "What would I have to work for?" fear of change or fear of the future.

How to Make Goals Work

Success is a very abstract word. Just as failure is a habit, so can success be, but you need to look at success in relative terms. You form success *habits* by openly acknowledging success even in minor areas. Purposely set goals in some areas where you have not felt successful. Planning will make them work.

Here are some suggestions:
- Learn to visualize yourself completing goals every single day.
- Speak in terms of "I have decided to" rather than "I have to."
- Talk in positive terms (this doesn't mean being a Pollyanna).
- Talk others and yourself up in positive terms.
- Project positive *self-control* by preparation and affirmative action steps.
- Focus on *the rewards of success*. When setting goals, be sure you define *your* benefit from succeeding.
- Talk of your goals in vivid and pictorial terms.
- Once you have committed your goals to paper, share them with someone who can help you achieve them.
- Think and act like a winner. Help others be winners.
- Restrict carrying out your goals to one day at a time for two weeks, and then go all out for a month.

START NOW!

CHAPTER THIRTEEN

Guideposts to Management

This chapter is both a review and a convenient reference for you. We have taken the salient points from each chapter and summarized them. However, it is important that each chapter be read carefully to gain the full benefit of the material presented.

CHAPTER ONE: *What Is Back-To-Basics Management?*

Today's business requires more than knowledge of techniques and technology. It demands that the managers understand the human aspect of management. Foundation block number one in back-to-basics management is:

News + information + comment	=	knowledge
Knowledge + thinking + feedback	=	understanding
Understanding + commitment + discipline	=	back-to-basics management

It is important for the back-to-basics manager to understand that knowledge is not enough for successful management in today's world, that this whole formula must be used for a completed cycle of success.

Foundation block number two is:

Effective communication. We can store and pass on information through the use of computers, but it is talking and listening to one another that is important. This communication must take place within a higher and more pragmatic area of management.

Foundation block number three is:

Interpersonal relationships. For this communication to be effective and management to be successful, the human aspect of interpersonal relations must be taken into consideration.

Back-to-basics management:
1. Recognizes natural talent.
2. Is anti-bureaucratic.
3. Disdains fear and greed as motivators in business.
4. Puts heavy emphasis on learned skills.
5. Recognizes the need for both instinct and non-conformity in thinking.
6. Is a compassionate person-to-person management style.
7. Is the perfect strategy for today's manager, who must use the new technologies with time-tested management principles.

The back-to-basics manager:
1. Knows himself.
2. Is an expert at getting things done.
3. Is skilled in time management and self-organization.
4. Uses communication as his prime management tool.
5. Is big on people skills.
6. Is creative and innovative and knows how to motivate and use the creative output of his people.
7. Knows how to delegate work successfully.
8. Is an effective supervisor.

CHAPTER TWO: *Creative Listening*

Listening is one of the most important skills a back-to-basics manager can learn. Forty-five percent of the time he spends in communication is spent listening. Without good listening habits a manager's effectiveness in using what he hears can drop below 25%. Listening is more than hearing words. It is understanding what is being said, what is not being said and what our motivation for listening is. Our motivation and emotions greatly influence our listening effectiveness.

The five blocks to effective listening are:
- Attempting to extract only the facts from a message
- Allowing certain words to affect us emotionally
- Rejecting what is being said because of our predisposition to the subject
- Looking and acting as if we are listening when we are not
- Criticizing what is being said because we dislike the speaker or his mannerisms.

Here's how to increase your listening effectiveness:
- Prepare yourself to listen.
- Listen to the speaker from his point of view.
- Concentrate on the major points and not the facts. Keep looking for information you can use.
- Build defense mechanisms against words that have emotionally laden meanings for you.
- Learn to keep an open mind. Look for the positive aspects of what is being said.
- Pay attention. Note how the talk is organized.
- Keep your mind on the speaker.
- Listen between the lines for information and ideas that may not have been put into words.
- Try to anticipate points and ideas.
- Review and weigh what you are hearing. This will help keep your mind from wandering.
- Withhold judgment, evaluation and decision until the speaker has finished.
- Ask silent mental questions about what is being said.
- Actively seek areas of interest for yourself in what is being said.
- Don't let note taking be a distraction.
- Adjust to distractions; don't just tolerate them.
- Exercise your mind. Learn to listen to technical information and expository material.
- Keep eye contact with the speaker (especially on a one-to-one basis).
- Listen with your whole person.

CHAPTER THREE: *Decision Making*

Decision making is the fundamental activity of managers. Even when a manager feels he does not have enough facts, he must act. Managers are constantly being presented with facts and information stated in words (verbal maps) on which they must base their decisions. To make effective decisions, managers must make sure that these "verbal maps" fit the actual territory or reality they are describing. A manager must always remember that people describe circumstances and events according to how they *interact* with the situation. Because of this the "facts" may not always be an accurate and adequate description of what is really going on.

A manager's judgmental thinking can be helped by remembering:
1. You can't possibly know everything about everything. Develop the habit of open-mindedness. Learn to use the phrase "as far as I know" in your thinking.
2. Learn to think in terms of degrees by silently adding the phrase "up to a point." This will help do away with either/or type of thinking.
3. Be analytical and honest. Try not to select things that prove only your point of view.
4. We see things not as they are, but *as we are.* When we speak in terms of good, large and other subjective adjectives, we are not describing qualities, but our personal reaction to the subject. Learn to incorporate the silent phrases "to me" . . . "to him" . . . "to her" . . . "to them" in your thinking.
5. Be careful in using common nouns such as house, dog, or manager. No two things are exactly alike. Oversimplified labels can lead us to erroneous conclusions.
6. Make sure you have the authority to make the needed decision.
7. A decision should be made by people as close as possible to the function it affects.
8. It is important that you train those you supervise in the art of making decisions. You should demand that they offer a partial solution, if not a full one, when they bring you a problem.
9. All decisions carry a risk factor.
10. All decisions bring changes you must be prepared to handle.

11. Don't spend time making decisions that you don't intend to carry out.

12. Before implementing decisions gather as much information as practical about the circumstances surrounding the decision.

13. When planning your implementation of the decision, make sure you have included all elements that *may* have to be handled.

14. In your planning make sure you have set alternative courses of action in case of obstacles or problems.

15. In communicating your decision remember the phrase "people are a resource" is a working reality for the back-to-basics manager.

16. Communicate your ideas, decisions, policy and values in such a manner that they elicit support and motivate.

17. Communicate decisions to those you report to first.

18. Plan your communication to your superior in such a manner that you totally inform him of all the surrounding facts and circumstances, as well as elicit his support.

19. Make sure you communicate with other departments that *may* be affected by your decision.

20. Try to include the employees whose work will be affected in both the decision-making and implementation plans.

21. Write, speak and communicate in language that motivates employees.

22. Show employees how the decisions will be to their benefit and why their participation is needed.

CHAPTER FOUR: *Managing Change*

Change is vital to the continuing growth of our society. One of your prime functions as a back-to-basics manager is to manage change and prepare your people for change. Most people see change as a fearsome proposition; they see it as instability.

However, people adjust to change more easily when they feel they have been instrumental in either the decision-making or the implementation process. Change is vital to the continuing growth of any organization. Because of this it is important to understand that change is what gives your company a competitive edge.

Keys to managing and understanding change are:

1. The more ingrained the routine or habit the harder it will be to change.
2. Consistency in your attitude about fundamentals will help your people during times of change.
3. Setting boundaries will help minimize feelings of instability during times of change.
4. Remain reliable in the eyes of your people during change, explaining the whys and wherefores of a change.
5. Be comfortable with change yourself.
6. Before initiating any change, explore your own reactions to the changing situation.
7. Routines and sameness (not systems) can cut down on productivity. Examine these areas for possible change.
8. Remember that each action you take in making a change will bring a reaction of some sort.
9. To the best of your ability know the reactions of all those who will be affected by change.
10. Be sure to consider the reactions of others to change when doing your implementation planning. (Don't forget to allow extra time for these reactions.)
11. Make sure you have provided for alternative courses of action in planning for change.

You should consider a change when:

1. It will give you an edge over the competition.
2. The change will be truly beneficial.
3. You feel that the ensuing reactions can be handled and will be beneficial.

Initiating a successful change requires these 6 steps:

1. Make a critical judgment and decision.
2. Motivate your people and all those involved.
3. Produce an action.
4. Find possible alternatives in case of problems.
5. Make sure your people learn how to relate to the new situation.
6. Be prepared to handle unforeseen consequences.

CHAPTER FIVE: *Managing Motivation*

A back-to-basics manager-leader must be able to show others how to meet their goals and needs in a work situation. Motivation is the inner drive of the individual that moves him to action to meet goals and needs. In order to manage motivation, you must understand the *how* and *why* of human interaction. By understanding human interaction you will be able to form (and change) attitudes and opinions, stimulate creativity, help your people learn and develop, manage conflict productively and master a host of other topics which are needed for effective human interaction and leadership. In back-to-basics management-leadership the individual is pre-eminent and not the task. As a manager, your performance will be judged by the performance and productivity of others. Your goal is to free yourself from detail and task-defined roles so that you can move up to the real challenge of leadership-managing and motivating people as individuals and in groups.

In understanding motivation it is important to remember that the reason anyone wants to accomplish anything is the benefit or the reward for completion of the task.

In managing motivation these points will help you:
1. The desire for the result of behavior is the driving force that produces behavior.
2. A benefit must be a benefit to the employee (not to the manager alone) in order to produce results.
3. A benefit or reward must tie in with a person's tangible and intangible needs.
4. Tangible needs are the substantive payoffs the person doing the job wants from the job.
5. Intangible needs are the reason why a person wants what he wants from the job.
6. Business job goals are specific and measurable and deal with objective matters.
7. Behavioral job goals are less measurable and involve changes in behavior or interpersonal skills that will help achieve a business goal.
8. We are all motivated all the time, because we tend to do those things we find rewarding.

9. Each of us tends to think of rewards in a different light. Thus it is your job to make the rewards fit the individual to accomplish the task.
10. When you link goals with needs you provide rewards that produce, job commitment.
11. Employees' needs (tangible and intangible) can be identified through their behavior and statements about career goals.
12. Employees' statements about their tangible needs give you clues to their intangible needs.
13. A performance appraisal conversation about every six months will keep you up to date on the changing motivational needs of your employees.
14. Because we cannot always meet an employee's tangible needs, it is important to try to meet his intangible needs.
15. Intangible need-motivation achieves the same level of motivation as tangible need-motivation.
16. When talking to your employees, speak the language of motivation; use such words as participation, opportunity, involvement and meaningfulness.
17. Always speak in terms of benefits to those you are trying to motivate.
18. In order to communicate and motivate, you must have a two-way dialogue.
19. Both you and your employee must be in the right receptive mood for a two-way dialogue to occur.
20. The back-to-basics manager-leader gets his employees involved strategically with decisions; delegates in a planned, purposeful manner; ties employees' needs to company goals and quotas; encourages analysis and criticism of what's going on.

CHAPTER SIX: *Managing Time*

The back-to-basics manager has a grasp of the psychological function of time and how to use it. Time has a direct relationship to productivity. The back-to-basics manager is conscious of the use of time and the quality of time spent. By upgrading and understanding your attitude toward time you can become more efficient.

Traditional time management tells us we must first:

1. Be selective and set priorities for our work.
2. Delegate and eliminate all the tasks we possibly can.

If you have done this and you still do not have time to produce as you should, then you must increase your capacity to discriminate and refine your tasks so that you can increase your output.

You can do this by forming very clear mental pictures of a situation. The clearer the picture the faster you can take action. The clearer the picture and more decisively and efficiently you can act with full energy.

Increase the clarity of your mental pictures by:

1. Increasing your alertness.
2. Increasing your available energy.
3. Increasing your knowledge and experience.

You can manage time more effectively by:

1. Being single-minded, keeping your attention on the task at hand.
2. Not allowing yourself to become preoccupied.
3. Remaining alert; not doing things habitually.
4. Changing routines and habits in order to stay alert.
5. Giving your mind challenges on a daily basis.
6. Learning new skills.
7. Taking 3 minutes out of every hour to refresh your mind and reset priorities.
8. Reviewing your day each night, looking for those times when you were not alert.
9. Setting specific times for daydreaming.
10. Being positive in your thinking and attitudes. Positive attitudes produce energy; negative attitudes reduce energy.
11. Learning to turn negative energy to positive energy in group meetings and individual encounters.
12. Ridding yourself of anxieties, fears, doubts and uncertainties, all of which use up your energy.
13. Learning to rid yourself of inner dialogues and "battles" which use up your energy.
14. Remembering that relaxation and receptivity increase alertness and energy.

15. Learning to rid yourself of stress and tension.
16. Allowing plenty of time for rest.
17. Exercising and keeping yourself physically fit.
18. Learning to see things in a different manner than you have in the past.
19. Knowing when to start and stop projects.
20. Learning to set priorities and delegate.
21. Learning to communicate effectively so that time is not wasted.
22. Learning to listen.
23. Learning to say no.
24. Learning how to handle interruptions so that they are not the main thrust of the day.
25. Learning when your best decision times, working times and creative times are.
26. Learning how to take time off.
27. Learning to make a time plan, with daily agendas, monthly calendars.
28. Learning to make a yearly plan and a five-year plan.
29. Remembering that attention and effort give projects and ideas value.
30. Knowing where and how you spend your time.
31. Doing the *right* things right.
32. Working smarter, not harder.
33. Always making sure you are solving the right problem.

CHAPTER SEVEN: *Managing Delegation*

Delegating is the art of being able to hand someone else a job you can do perfectly well. To be efficient, a manager must decentralize his job through delegation. A manager's job is to supervise—not to do—the tasks. Research shows that the most successful managers are those who continue to manage during times of crisis, rather than rolling up their sleeves and doing the work themselves. As a back-to-basics manager you must make a conscious effort to select those tasks which you alone must do. Many managers have trouble delegating because of their internal feelings about delegation. They feel they may lose something, such as power or authority. In order to delegate efficiently you must gain control of these inner feelings and doubts.

When you delegate, you:
1. Free up your available time.
2. Multiply your energy.
3. Let those under you develop their skills.
4. Make time for leadership development.
5. Make time for innovative ideas that keep you ahead of the competition.
6. Find out whom you can trust to carry out projects.

In order to delegate successfully, you must:
1. State policy clearly and explicitly.
2. Define the tasks to be delegated precisely.
3. Have job descriptions for employees.
4. Communicate the task so that the employees understand how it fits in with their job description.
5. Set goals and objectives for each task.
6. Make sure employees understand the task and are motivated to complete it.
7. Set controls so that you know the task is being completed.
8. Let the employees do things their own way, in a manner that is comfortable for them.
9. Make a plan for each task that can and should be delegated.
10. Look at each task as if you were unfamiliar with it.
11. Encourage employees to make decisions and solve problems.
12. Ask employees to suggest solutions (even if the solutions won't work) whenever they present a problem.
13. Set up check points so that major pitfalls can be avoided.
14. Review each uncompleted task, looking for the causes of the breakdown in the system. Take this information into consideration when delegating the next task.
15. Make sure that both you and your employees can see and understand the results of the tasks which have been delegated.
16. Learn to use planning tools, daily agendas and tickler files; encourage employees to do the same.
17. Remember that your managerial success depends on your ability to direct others.

CHAPTER EIGHT: *Leadership*

You can be given the title of manager, but you cannot be given leadership. In order to be a leader, you must demonstrate your leadership ability to those you are leading and managing. You must be willing to accept the responsibility of leadership. You must be willing to accept and use the power that comes with a leadership role. To be successful you must show employees how to achieve what they want. Leadership is a matter of degrees. It does not happen all at once and many of the successful leadership characteristics are learned ones. As a leader you will have the power to shape and mold the present and future through the cooperation of a group. You will act as a role model to those in the group.

To be a leader, you must:
1. Have a voluntary following.
2. Demonstrate to your following that you can help them achieve their goals and are the best person available for this task.
3. Understand the weaknesses and strengths of yourself and your following.
4. Accept responsibility.
5. Be willing to accept power without undue reluctance or zeal.
6. Use power without abusing it.
7. Have the ability to motivate others.
8. Have the ability to achieve your own goals.
9. Form premises that lead to useful conclusions.
10. Continue learning and growing in your own skills as a leader.
11. Delegate successfully.
12. Help your people to participate in decisions which affect them.
13. Be non-punitive.
14. Communicate and encourage two-way communications.
15. Show pride in your people and their performance to maintain high morale.
16. Be able to plan both short- and long-term projects successfully.
17. Be able to sustain your leadership role in times of crisis.

18. Know that each individual counts and that each one can, if properly motivated, make a specific contribution.

CHAPTER NINE: *Body Language*

It is the person receiving your communication who makes what you say or do valuable. Without a receiver you are only uttering sounds. When you communicate, you are always dealing with the perception of each individual. Because of this what is not said and what we do with gestures, tone of voice and the entire environment must be thought of as part of the communication process.

To better understand this process:
1. Learn to read the body language of yourself and others.
2. Know that body gestures and language should reinforce each other.
3. Learn to listen and observe others.
4. When observing others, keep in mind their body gestures, eye motions, skin/touch sensations (how does their hand feel when you shake it). How do they deal with the space around them?
5. Learn to process all the signals from the silent languages to get an accurate reading.
6. Remember that some signals may have more than one meaning. It is the entire picture that gives a true reading.
7. Remember that we give different signals in different settings.
8. Remember that a signal may change its meaning according to the setting.
9. Learn body language at a conscious level.

CHAPTER TEN: *Managerial Coaching and Training*

Coaching and training are a never ending process for the back-to-basics manager. Whether you are conducting a formal training course or explaining a task one-on-one to an employee, you must have a knowledge of how to train. In learning to train others you must start by understanding how people learn and how the mind works. No matter what the training or coaching situation, the following must be understood for you to be successful at this task:

1. We learn by two main methods: rote memory and experience/association.
2. Experience/association has been found to be the most effective.
3. A person must participate in the activity in order to learn.
4. We must be able to articulate and relate knowledge in a pragmatic sense in order to retain or use it effectively.
5. The mind works in an orderly fashion when gaining and relating information.
6. The mind works in three steps: (1) it gathers facts and experiences, (2) it relates and associates this information to previous information, (3) it draws a working conclusion on which action is based.
7. If, in step one, the facts and experiences are erroneous in nature, the conclusion will be erroneous.
8. Once you accomplish steps 1 and 2, the mind will inevitably reach a conclusion.
9. Keep your statement of facts short and to the point and introduce only one fact at a time.
10. Your association statement should show how information is to be used.
11. Have employees verbalize their conclusions.
12. Be aware of learning blocks in employees.
13. Try to state information in such a way that you help employees draw mental pictures.
14. Try to present information so that it relates to the current work situation.
15. Remember that 80% of our learning is visual.
16. Use universal analogies and metaphors.
17. Find common points of understanding.
18. Try not to speak in terms of good or bad; avoid judgment blocks that lead employees to fear making mistakes.
19. Keep the atmosphere open and relaxed.
20. Use circles and horseshoe sitting arrangements when training a group.
21. Come from behind your desk in a one-on-one basis.
22. Remember that the normal attention span is very limited.
23. Speak clearly and use voice modulation and body gestures to help make points.
24. Encourage trial-and-error conversation.

25. When counseling and coaching reinforce effective behavior by helping employees be aware of their strengths.
26. Let employees know where improvement is needed and show them how you can help them.
27. Help employees see the relationship between their needs and those of the company.

CHAPTER ELEVEN: *Communication Skills*

Effective communication is central to everything a back-to-basics manager does. Human interaction succeeds or fails as a direct result of our ability to communicate. Communication is a process composed of five links: Who? Says what? To whom? Through what medium? With what effect? Communication is inseparable from your total behavior as a manager.

To be a more effective communicator:
1. Create a climate in which you have a strong relationship with your employees.
2. Make building this climate one of your primary responsibilities.
3. Avoid the tendency to communicate because of your title.
4. Try to adopt the employee's frame of reference.
5. Be mindful of other points of view.
6. Remember that you are trying to develop a team which will achieve mutual goals.
7. Remember that the listener decides if he wants to listen, read or be motivated; shape your communication accordingly.
8. Use words to transmit ideas and information. People give meaning to the words.
9. Remember that no two people ever grasp a meaning in exactly the same way.
10. Ask these six questions before each communication:
    a. What do I intend to communicate?
    b. What will I actually communicate?
    c. What do I really mean, and what will be the emotional impact of the communication?
    d. What does the receiver of the communication expect to hear?
    e. What might he hear, despite what is being said?

     f. How will he feel about what he hears?

11. Remember that communication is a two-way process.

12. In order to communicate effectively not only must you be understood, but you must also have generated a desired action.

13. Present one idea at a time; make the statement; develop the idea; restate the idea; call to action.

14. Say what you have to say simply.

15. Make your statements brief.

16. Use words that draw mental pictures for those listening and reading.

17. Get acceptance of one idea before moving on to the next.

18. As a listener, be responsive to emotions, encourage expression, sympathize and empathize, and give of yourself to the speaker.

19. In written communication, command the attention of the reader.

20. Think of your reading audience as one person, to achieve a more personal touch.

21. In writing memos, try the direct-mail formula:
- Promise a benefit
- Enlarge on the benefit
- Tell the reader specifically what he will get
- Go into detail, backing up your promises with proof
- Tell the reader what he might lose if he doesn't act *now*
- Rephrase your reader benefit
- Incite to action *now*!

22. Make sure your ideas are in logical order.

23. Use copywriters' attention getting devices:
- underline
- CAPITALIZE
- Indent imaginatively
- Punctuate (e.g. use parentheses)
- Use exclamation points for extra emphasis!

24. Before sending a letter ask yourself;
- Is it reader-oriented?
- Is it tactful?

- Is is clear and concise?
- Is it conversational?
- Is is helpful?
- Have you created good will?

If the answer to each question is yes, send the letter.

25. When running a meeting, remember that it gives participants a chance to develop into a team.
26. Have a specific purpose in mind when calling a meeting.
27. Don't call a meeting if the matter can be handled in some other way.
28. Make the purpose of the meeting known beforehand.
29. Invite only those who are needed in the meeting.
30. Start at the time announced.
31. Stop when the purpose of the meeting has been achieved.
32. Prepare your agenda in advance.
33. Keep to your agenda.
34. Schedule far enough in advance so everyone can think about the purpose.
35. Ask questions—that's the easiest way to get a discussion going.
36. Learn to handle members who dominate a meeting by fielding questions to others in the group.
37. Ask members who do not participate direct, specific questions.
38. Bring the discussion back to the point with questions.
39. Do not take sides when conflict occurs.
40. Remind the group during conflict that intelligent people have different opinions.
41. Use humor to relieve tensions.
42. When you make a mistake, admit it and laugh at yourself, ask the group for help and try something else.
43. Use Robert's "Rules of Order" to reach a conclusion.
44. Listen better than anyone else.
45. Adjourn on time.

CHAPTER TWELVE: *Managerial Goal Setting*

Goals are internalized dreams; plans and objectives are means to accomplish goals. The back-to-basics manager must know how to set goals for himself and for his employees and how to make appropriate plans to reach those goals and objectives. Research shows that you must have a clear picture in your mind of what you want to achieve and that both goals and plans must be written to be carried out successfully. Most managers understand the importance of planning, but a lack of organization keeps them from doing the extensive planning that would give them a competitive edge.

In setting goals and planning your first step is to become organized:

1. Make sure you have formal job descriptions for yourself and for your employees.
2. Identify every task, function and time-consuming act.
3. Become aware of what must be done on a daily, bi-weekly, weekly, bi-monthly, monthly, quarterly, semi-annual and annual basis.
4. Establish how long each task takes to complete without interruptions.
5. Remember that being organized is a learned skill that takes self-discipline and the breaking of old habits.
6. Clean house, making sure your whole office is well-organized from the files to the top of your desk.
7. Write down each task you are responsible for in a yearly planning calendar on the date it is due . . . plus the date it should be started to be completed on time.
8. Every manager must handle interruptions and emergencies. The key is not to deviate too long from your plan.
9. Leave your work area clean whenever you will be out of the office and urge that employees do the same.
10. Insist that all files, equipment and other items be put in their proper place immediately after use.
11. Twice a month check to make sure all files and information are where they should be.
12. It takes 21 days to break or make habits and may take you as long as 6 months to become truly organized.
13. Make sure your personal life is in order.
14. Learn to say no and explain why if you are asked to take on tasks outside of your normal duties.
15. Remember, at any time, anyone should be able to step into your job without confusion. Business cannot afford to keep people who make themselves indispensable.

Once you are organized your next step is to start setting goals and objectives and making plans to carry them out:

1. Start by taking a good look at your personal goals and business goals. Do they mesh?
2. Form a mental picture of where you would like to be at retirement, both personally and financially.
3. Set goals and objectives within specific time frames.
4. Make a list of what must be done in order to achieve each goal and objective.
5. Remember the more detail you give your planning the easier it will be to achieve the goal.
6. Make sure you have a starting date and a completion date in your plan for each step necessary to complete goals and objectives.
7. At the end of each day fill out a list of what must be done for the coming day.
8. Make a notation on each item that can be delegated and to whom it should go.
9. Leave nothing to memory in your daily planning.
10. Check your list the first thing in the morning before leaving for the office.
11. Take 3 to 5 minutes each hour to clear your head and check off your list. Reset priorities if necessary, based on finished projects and incoming information.
12. Make sure you can easily identify long-term projects on your daily list.
13. Make a monthly plan and agenda.
14. Add at least three hours a week for exercise (not weekend time) to your weekly planning schedule.

If you are having difficulty reaching goals and objectives, are you:

1. Making your daily agenda too long and impossible to complete?
2. Not setting priorities or seeing too many areas as priorities?
3. Experiencing the non-completion syndrome, not being able to finish even small tasks? Start with a small area and force yourself to finish it. Work up if necessary.
4. Unable to visualize yourself finishing a task or completing your goals?

5. Experiencing a lack of self-esteem, self-confidence, self-motivaton, self-discipline?
6. Experiencing a fear of success?

Make sure you see failure in degrees and point out your successes.

To make your goals work:
1. Form success habits by openly acknowledging the completion of even minor goals.
2. Learn to visualize yourself completing your objectives each day.
3. Speak in positive and decisive terms about your goals and objectives.
4. Project positive *self-control* by preparation and affirmative action steps.
5. Focus on the rewards of success. Be sure to define the benefit you will get by completing a goal.
6. Talk of goals and objectives in vivid and pictorial terms.
7. Think and act like a winner.
8. Dedicate yourself to carrying out your plans and goals one day at a time for 2 weeks, and then go all out for a month.

Let us summarize the fundamental qualities of the back-to-basics manager:

- Recognizes the essential humanity of everyone with whom he is associated—accepting them as warm, feeling, caring human beings
- Believes and trusts people—and tells them his own feelings towards them
- Expects them to become all they are capable of—and is ready to help them on the way
- Works with them to establish sound goals and convert their ideas into reality
- Helps them to use time efficiently
- Points out what the organization expects from them through clear statements of company policy
- Helps them develop the self-discipline needed to identify and achieve their potential
- Understands that effective communication is motivation; keeps the communication network open at all times

- Delegates responsibility
- Supports his people in their decisions
- Praises good performance and helps people correct their mistakes by working with them on a one-to-one basis
- Responds to people's needs
- Understands that the optimal use of his managerial skills fulfills his economic responsibility to the company
- Is fully cognizant of today's business ethics and understands the need for all participants to gain some good from every business relationship

To sum up, the back-to-basics manager has an optimistic view of people. He builds on cooperation rather than competition. He deals with all aspects of business in ways that reflect appreciation for people. He understands and appreciates the human relationships within an organization and is aware of the relationships between his organization, its people and the outside world.

We think the lessons to be learned are not only "basic" but absolutely essential. We feel back-to-basics management fits right into current business practice, and certainly into the evolving role of the American corporation.

Organizations are only what people make them. Remember that, and the authors will feel they have achieved their objective. And you will be better equipped to achieve your personal objectives in management.

Bibliography

CHAPTER ONE

Aristotle, *Man In the Universe,* various publishers.

Barnard, C. *Functions of the Executive.* Cambridge, Mass.: Harvard University Press, 1968.

Blake, Robert R. and Mouton, Jane Srygley, *Productivity; The Human Side.* N.Y.: Amacom, 1981.

Chase, Stuart. *The Proper Study of Mankind.* N.Y.: Harper and Row, 1963.

Drucker, Peter F. *The Effective Executive.* N.Y.: Harper and Row, 1967.

Filley, Alan C. *The Compleat Manager: What Works When.* Champaign, Ill.: Research Press Co., 1978.

Foreign Policy Assoc. *Toward the Year 2018.* N.Y.: Cowles Educational Corp., 1968.

Harris, Sydney J. *The Authentic Person.* Niles, Ill.: Argus Communications, 1972.

Harvard Business Review on Human Relations, N.Y.: Harper and Row, 1959.

Herzberg, Fredrick. *Work and the Nature of Man.* Cleveland, Ohio: World, 1961.

Humble, John W. *How to Manage by Objectives.* N.Y.: Amacom, 1978.

Jay, Anthony. *Management and Machiavelli.* N.Y.: Holt, Rinehart and Winston, 1967.

Laing, R.D. *The Divided Self.* Chicago: Quadrangle Books, 1960.

Levinson, Harry. *The Exceptional Executive.* Cambridge, Mass: Harvard University Press, 1969.

Likert, Rensis. *The Human Organization.* N.Y.: McGraw-Hill, 1967.

Maccoby, Michael. *The Gamesman.* N.Y.: Simon and Schuster, 1976.

Maren, Norman. *Psychology in Industry.* Boston: Houghton Mifflin 1955.

Marrow, Alfred J. *Behind the Executive Mask.* N.Y.: American Management Association, 1964.

Masuda, Yoneji. *The Information Society.* Tokyo: Institute for the Information Society, 1981.

McClelland, D.C., Atkinson, J.W., Clark, R.A., and Lowell, E.L., *The Achieving Society.* Princeton, N.J. Van Nostrand, 1961.

Miles, Raymond. *Theories of Management.* N.Y.: McGraw-Hill, 1975.

Mitton, Daryl G. and Mitton, Betty L. *Managerial Clout.* Englewood Cliffs, N.J.: Prentice-Hall, 1980.

Pascarella, Perry. *Humanagement in the Future Corporation.* N.Y.: Van Nostrand Reinhold Co., 1981.

Peter, L.J. and Hull, R. *The Peter Principle.* N.Y.: William Morrow, 1969

Reisman, David. *The Lonely Crowd: a Study of the Changing American Character.* New Haven: Yale University Press, 1950.

Rush, H.M. *Behavioral Science Concepts and Management Applications.* N.Y.: The Conference Board, Inc., 1969.

Sloma, Richard S. *How to Measure Managerial Performance.* N.Y.: Macmillan, 1980.

Thompson, James D. *Organizations in Action.* N.Y.: McGraw-Hill, 1964.

Townsend, Robert. *Up the Organization.* N.Y.: Alfred Knopf, 1970.

Whyte, W.H. *The Organization Man.* N.Y.: Simon and Schuster, 1956.

Wiener, Norbert. *The Human Use of Human Beings.* Garden City, N.Y.: Doubleday-Anchor, 1956.

Wren, Daniel A. *The Evolution of Management Thought.* N.Y.: Ronald Press, 1972.

CHAPTER TWO

Johnson, Wendell. *People in Quandries.* N.J.: Harper & Bros., 1946.

_____ . *Your Most Enchanted Listener.* N.Y.: Harper & Bros., 1956.

McLuhan, M. *Understanding the Media: the Extensions of Man.* N.Y.: McGraw-Hill, 1965.

Nichols, Ralph G. and Stevens, Leonard A. *Are You Listening?* N.Y.: McGraw-Hill, 1967

_____ . "Listening to People," *Harvard Business Review.* Vol. 35, no. 5., 1957.

Singer, Jerome L. and Switzer, Ellen. *Mind Play.* Englewood Cliffs, N.J.: Prentice-Hall, 1980.

Sommer, R. *Personal Space.* Englewood Cliffs, N.J.: Prentice-Hall, 1969.

CHAPTER THREE

Brinker, Henry. *Decision-Making: Creativity, Judgement and Systems.* Columbus, Ohio: Ohio State University Press, 1972.

Bross, Irwin. *Design for Decision.* N.Y.: Macmillan, 1953.

Davis, Creath. *How to Win in a Crisis.* Grand Rapids, Mich.: Zondervan, 1976.

Filley, A.C. *Interpersonal Conflict Resolution.* Glenview, Ill.: Scott, Foresman, 1975.

Janis, Irving and Mann, Leon. *Decision-Making.* N.Y.: Free Press, 1977.

Keyes, K.S. *How to Develop Your Thinking Ability.* N.Y.: McGraw-Hill, 1950.

Maier, N.R.F. *Problem Solving and Creativity in Individuals and Groups.* Monterey, Calif.: Brooks-Cole, 1970.

Randolph, Robert M. *Planagement: Moving Concept into Reality.* N.Y.: Amacom, 1975.

Reilly, William J. *Straight Thinking.* N.Y.: Harper & Bros., 1935.

Simon, Herbert A. *The New Science of Management Decision.* Englewood Cliffs, N.J.: Prentice-Hall, 1977.

Steiner, I.D. *Group Process and Productivity.* N.Y.: Academic Press, 1972.

CHAPTER FOUR

Bennis, W.G. *Changing Organizations.* N.Y.: McGraw-Hill, 1966.

Ewing, Davis W. *The Human Side of Planning.* N.Y.: Macmillan, 1969.

Hoffer, Eric. *The Ordeal of Change.* N.Y.: Harper and Row, 1963.

Huse, Edgar F. *Organization Development and Change.* St. Paul, Minn.: West Publishing Co., 1975.

May, Rollo. *The Courage to Create.* N.Y.: Bantam, 1975.

Rogers, Everett and Shoemaker, Floyd. *Communications of Innovations: A Cross-Cultural Approach.* N.Y.: Free Press, 1971.

Satir, Virginia. *People-making.* Palo Alto, Calif.: Science & Behavior Books, 1972.

Steiner, George A. *Top Management Planning.* N.Y.: Macmillan, 1969.

Zaltman, Gerald, Duncan, Robert and Holbek, Jonni. *Innovations and Organizations.* N.Y.: Wiley, 1973.

CHAPTER FIVE

Atkinson, J.W. and Feather, N.T. *A Theory of Achievement Motivation.* N.Y.: John Wiley and Sons, 1966.

Biderman, A.D. and Zimmer, H. *The Manipulation of Human Behavior.* N.Y.: John Wiley and Sons, 1961.

Blake, Robert R., Shepard, Herbert A., and Mouton, Jane S., *Managing Intergroup Conflict in Industry.* Houston, Texas: Gulf Publishing Co., 1965.

Dichter, Ernst. *The Strategy of Desire.* Garden City, N.Y.: Doubleday and Co.

Ford, Robert N. *Motivation Through the Work Itself.* N.Y.: Amacom, 1969.

Ivancevich, John M., Szilagyi, Andrew D. and Wallace, Marc J., *Organizational Behavior and Performance.* Santa Monica, Calif.: Goodyear Publishing Co., 1977.

Kolasa, B.J. *Introduction to Behavioral Science for Business.* N.Y.: John Wiley and Sons, 1969.

Kotten, John P. *Power in Management.* N.Y.: Amacom, 1947.

Leavitt, H.J. *Managerial Psychology.* Chicago: University of Chicago Press, 1958.

Lefton, Robert E., Buzzotta, V.R., Sherberg, Manuel and Karraker, Dean L. *Effective Motivation Through Performance Appraisal.* N.Y.: John Wiley and Sons, 1977.

Maslow, Abraham. "A Theory of Motivation," *Psychological Bulletin 50,* July 1943.

_____ . *Towards a Psychology of Being.* N.Y.: D. Nostrand Co., 1968.

McClelland, D.C. and Winter, D.G. *Motivating Economic Achievement.* N.Y.: Free Press, 1969.

Rogers, Carl R. *On Becoming a Person.* Boston: Houghton Mifflin, 1961.

Sharpe, Robert and Lewis, David. *The Success Factor.* N.Y.: Crown Publishers, 1976.

Steers, R.M. and Porter, L.W. *Motivation and Work Behavior.* N.Y.: McGraw-Hill, 1975.

Vroom, V.H. *Work and Motivation:* N.Y.: John Wiley and Sons, 1964.

Worthy, James C. "Factors Influencing Employee Morale," *Harvard Business Review,* Vol. 28, No. 1, Jan. 1950.

CHAPTER SIX

Bolton, Robert. *People Skills.* Englewood Cliffs, N.J.: Prentice-Hall, 1979.

Cooper, Joseph D. *How To Get More Done in Less Time.* Garden City, N.Y.: Doubleday, 1962.

Edwards, Joseph Dean. *Executives: Making Them Click.* N.Y.: University Books, 1956.

Gallway, W. Timothy. *Inner Tennis.* N.Y.: Random House, 1976.

McCay, James T. *The Management of Time.* Englewood Cliffs, N.J.: Prentice-Hall, 1959.

Mackenzie, R. Alec. *The Time Trap.* Amacom, 1972.

Nicoll, Maurice. *Living Time and the Integration of the Life.* London: Watkins, 1952.

CHAPTER SEVEN

Kemp, C.G. *Perspectives on Group Process.* Boston: Houghton Mifflin, 1964.

Leavitt, Harold. *Managerial Psychology.* 4th Edition. Chicago: University of Chicago Press, 1978.

Lifton, Walter M. *Groups: Facilitating Individual Growth and Social Change.* N.Y.: John Wiley and Sons, Inc., 1972.

Mabry, Edward A. and Barnes, Richard E. *The Dynamics of Small Group Communication.* Englewood Cliffs, N.J.: Prentice-Hall, 1980.

Maier, N.R.F., Solem, A. and Maier, A.A. *Supervisory and Executive Development.* N.Y.: John Wiley and Sons, Inc., 1957.

CHAPTER EIGHT

Fiedler, F. *A Theory of Leadership Effectiveness.* N.Y.: McGraw-Hill, 1967.

Fiedler, Fred E. and Chemers, M.M. *Leadership and Effective Management.* Glenview, Ill.: Scott Foresman, 1974.

Griffin, K. and Barnes, R.E. *Trusting Me, Trusting You.* Columbus, Ohio: Chas. E. Merrill, 1976.

Hollander, E.P. *Leaders Groups, and Influence.* N.Y.: Oxford University Press, 1964.

Likert, Rensis *The Human Organization.* N.Y.: McGraw-Hill, 1970.

Maccoby, Michael. *The Leader.* N.Y.: Simon and Schuster, 1981.

Rogers, Carl. *On Personal Power.* N.Y.: Delacorte Press, 1977.

Smith, Henry C. *Sensitivity to People*. N.Y.: McGraw-Hill, 1966.

Steiner, Gary A. *The Creative Organization*. Chicago: University of Chicago Press, 1965.

Stogdall, Ralph M. *Handbook of Leadership*. N.Y.: Free Press, 1974.

Tannenbaum, R., Weschler, I.R. and Massorik, F. *Leadership and Organization*. N.Y.: McGraw-Hill, 1961.

Toffler, Alvin. *Future Shock*. N.Y.: Random House, 1970.

_____ . *The Third Wave*. N.Y.: William Morrow and Company, 1980.

Walker, Stuart H. *Winning: The Psychology of Competition*. N.Y.: W.W. Norton, 1980.

CHAPTER NINE

Blier, Ernst G. and Valens, Evans G. *People Reading*. N.Y.: Warner Books, 1975.

Longfellow, Lawe A., Rose, Anthony, Van Orshoven, Terry, and Thommes, Martin. *Body Talk*. Del Mar, Calif. Communication/Research/Machines/Inc., 1970.

Morris, Desmond. *Intimate Behaviour*. N.Y.: Bantam Books. 1973.

Nierenberg, Gerald I. and Calero, Henry H. *How to Read a Person Like a Book*. N.Y.: Cornerstone Library, 1972.

Schafler, Albert E. and Schafler, Alice. *Body Language and Social Order*. Englewood Cliffs, N.J.: Prentice-Hall, 1972.

Shostrom, Everett L. *Man the Manipulator*. N.Y.: Bantam Books, 1968.

CHAPTER TEN

Blake, Robert J. and Mouton, Jane S. *Building A Dynamic Corporation Through Grid Organization Development*. Reading, Mass: Addison-Wesley, 1969.

Bors, J.S. *Explorations In Awareness*. N.Y.: Harper and Row, 1957.

Drucker, Peter F. *People and Performance*. N.Y.: Harper's College Press, 1977.

Lewis, David and Greene, James. *Thinking Better*. N.Y.: Rawson, Ware, Publishers, Inc. 1982.

McGregor, D. *The Professional Manager*. N.Y.: McGraw-Hill, 1967.

Menninger, Karl A. *The Human Mind*. N.Y.: Harper and Row, 1971.

Osborne, Alex F. *Applied Imagination*. N.Y.: Charles Scribner's Sons, 1953.

Sayles, Leonard. *Managerial Behavior at Work*. N.Y.: McGraw-Hill, 1972.

Shaw, M.E. *Group Dynamics: the Dynamics of Small Group Behavior*. N.Y.: McGraw-Hill, 1971.

Stogdell, R.M. *Individual Behavior and Group Achievement*. London: Oxford University Press, 1959.

Strauss, George and Sayles, Leonard R. *Behavioral Strategies for Managers*. Englewood Cliffs, N.J.: Prentice-Hall, 1980.

Wilson, Harold G. *Organizations Are People*. North Quincy, Mass: Christopher Publishing House, 1979.

CHAPTER ELEVEN

Bernays, Edward L. *The Engineering of Consent*. Norman: University of Oklahoma Press, 1955.

Bryson, Lyman. *The Communication of Ideas*. N.Y.: Harper and Bros., 1948.

Buzzotta, V.R., Lefton, R.E., and Sherberg, Manuel. *Effective Selling Through Psychology.* N.Y.: Wiley Interscience, 1972.

Carpenter, Edmund and McLuhan, Marshall, eds. *Explorations in Communication.* Boston: Beacon Press, 1960.

Donaldson, Les. *How to Use Psychological Leverage to Double the Power of What You Say.* West Nyack, N.Y.: Parker Publishing Co., 1978.

Harrison, Randall P. *Beyond Words.* Englewood Cliffs, N.J.: Prentice-Hall, 1974.

Hayakawa, S.I. *Language in Action.* N.Y.: Harcourt, Brace, and Co., 1940.

Lesly, Philip. *How We Discommunicate.* N.Y.: Amacom, 1979.

Makay, John J. and Sawyer, Thomas C. *Speech Communication Now!* Columbus, Ohio: Charles E. Merrill Publishing Co., 1973.

Myers, Gail E. *The Dynamics of Human Communication.* N.Y.: McGraw-Hill, 1973.

Oliver, Robert T., Zeller, Harold P. and Holtzman, Paul D. *Communicative Speaking and Listening.* N.Y.: Holt, Rinehart, and Winston Inc., 1968.

Peters, Raymond. *Communication Within Industry.* N.Y.: Harper & Bros., 1962.

Postman, Neil. *Crazy Talk, Stupid Talk.* N.Y.: Dell Publishing Co., Inc., 1976.

Robbins, James G. and Jones, Barbara S. *Effective Communication for Today's Manager.* N.Y.: Lebhar-Friedman, 1976.

Safire, William. *On Language.* N.Y.: Times Books, 1980.

Simmons, Harry. *How to Talk Your Way to Success.* N.Y. Castle Books, 1954.

Van Fleet, James K. *Power with People.* West Nyack, N.Y.: Parker Publishing Co., 1970.

Vardaman, George T., Halterman, Carroll C. and Vardaman, Patricia Black. *Cutting Communication Costs and Increasing Impacts.* N.Y.: John Wiley and Sons, Inc., 1970.

CHAPTER TWELVE

Campbell, John K., et al. *Managerial Performance and Effectiveness.* N.Y.: McGraw-Hill, 1970.

Chapple, E.N. and Sayles, L.R. *The Measurement of Management.* N.Y.: Macmillan, 1961.

Drucker, Peter R. *Management Tasks, Responsibilities, Practices.* N.Y.: Harper and Row, 1973.

Herzberg, F., Mausner, B., and Snydeman, B. *The Motivation to Work.* N.Y.: John Wiley, 1959.

Hughes, Charles L. *Goal Setting.* N.Y.: Amacom, 1965.

McFarland, Dalton E. *Managerial Achievement: Action Strategies.* Englewood Cliffs, N.J.: Prentice-Hall, 1977.

Zaleznik, A., and Moment, D. *The Dynamics of Interpersonal Behavior.* N.Y.: John Wiley, 1964.

Index